Ashlyi

A Journey of Faith, Hope, Perseverance, Justice, Triumph, and Forgiveness

LISA JOHNSON

All Scripture quotations are taken from the the New International Version, copyright 1973, 1978, 1984, by International Bible Society.

DEDICATION

This book is dedicated to those whose stories remain untold.

LISA JOHNSON

CONTENTS

ACKNOWLEDGMENTS

Ashlyn, my sweet baby girl, thank you for allowing me, and even encouraging me, to share your story. Your courage and selflessness are inspiring and have made a positive impact in the lives of others. I love you!

Alayna and Aiden, my Layna Bunny and big guy, thank you for being so understanding about the attention I have focused on Ashlyn's story, during the actual experience, while helping others since the experience, and during the journey of writing this book. I love you!

Zane, you're still so young and don't really have a clue about all that's transpired, but know that I love you!

Gregg, thank you for your unyielding support. I know you know how much I hate the saying, "You are my rock." But *you really are my rock*. This book was possible because you believed in me and encouraged me to fulfill this project. Thank you for listening to me talk about "the book" *every. single. day*. I love you!

Darla, thank you for being on this journey with me. I love you!

To all the people who shared your stories with me, thank you. You are the ones who kept me focused and motivated and gave me momentum to complete this project. Our story is your story.

Joel Kelley, thank you for your beautiful work on the cover! (Joel can be reached via JDKdesign@me.com.)

Employees and volunteers of Family and Children's Service (FCS), Child Abuse Network (CAN), Court Appointed Special Advocates (CASA), and Domestic Violence and Intervention Services (DVIS) - Thank you for serving children and families during incredibly scary and overwhelming circumstances. You have made, are making, and will continue to make an incredible difference in families!

Bikers Against Child Abuse (BACA) - Thank you for volunteering your time and resources to children impacted by abuse. I will be forever grateful to you all.

Lastly and most importantly, I am so thankful to God. He gave me the vision for this book. He's the author (except for a few not-so-nice words I threw in) and I'm simply the vessel. I'm thankful for the healing He's done in our lives. And I'm thankful for the paths He's created for us to share our story to help others.

FOREWARD

Over four years ago, I felt prompted to write this book. The vision I had for this book was to help others who have stories similar to ours to overcome hurts, failures, and disappointments. However, the journey of writing this book has helped me heal from this tragedy involving my daughter, Ashlyn. And while writing this book, I've been able to share my story and Ashlyn's story to help others - even before the book was completed.

I've chosen to approach mistakes I've made as learning experiences and not as regrets - except one. There is one decision I do regret.

However, I know that God doesn't waste a hurt. I've had plenty. And this book encompasses several of those.

Two things I've learned over the course of my almost 40 years of life include not ever saying "never" and not judging others' choices because we truly don't ever know how we would react or respond in any given situation until we find ourselves in it.

Please read this book with an open heart and open mind. My goal is that you find hope and encouragement through our journey.

I welcome you to share how this book has impacted you via Ashlyn's Story Facebook page: https://www.facebook.com/AshlynTheStory and via Twitter @LisaThePro.

Some names and identifying details have been changed to protect the privacy of individuals.

1 INNOCENT BEGINNINGS

My parents met in 1971 during their junior year at Mojave High School in Mojave, California. Their first date was the Junior/Senior prom. One day in class, my mom mentioned having a prom dress, but no date. My dad, doing his best friend a favor, was dressing up for prom just to go pick up his best friend's date. His friend was of Hispanic descent, however his girlfriend's parents would not allow her to date boys of Hispanic descent. After picking up "his date," the plan was for my dad to drop her off with his best friend. Since my dad didn't "officially" have a date and my mom needed a date, my dad quickly drafted a note asking her to prom and passed her the note in class. She still has that note to this day.

After their first date, it was set; they were an item. They dated for about a year before my dad proposed, marrying in the month of July just after graduating from high school. Eleven months later, they welcomed their first child, my older sister. A few years later, they relocated to Lawton, Oklahoma where my dad was stationed in the Army. Catoosa, a suburb of Tulsa, was their following relocation. Catoosa is the city where I grew up.

My upbringing was quite normal and routine. Unlike many parents in that day, mine were married and they still are. There were three kids in our family, of which I am the middle child of three girls. Family was and always has been important to my parents and grandparents; family came before anything except my dad's job. My dad worked hard to provide for us. Monday through Friday, he got up at 4:00 a.m. and began work at 5:00 a.m., and he finished work at 4:30 p.m. everyday of the week. On Saturdays, he worked from 5:00 a.m. until noon. A good company man, my dad has been loyal and the company has been great to him! This year, he celebrates 38 years with that organization.

My mom was able to stay at home with us due to my parents' conservative and thrifty spending habits. Although she occasionally chose to work a few jobs outside the home, for the most part she was at home with us. Even though my mom was home more than my dad, my dad was the primary disciplinarian. When we were in trouble, I remember mom saying, "Just wait until your dad gets home!" Who doesn't remember their mom saying that!?! I remember thinking, "Well, you're just as much a parent as he is. Why don't you just take care of it?" I had just as many opinionated thoughts then as I do now, but luckily I chose to not actually verbalize those thoughts in my younger years! I rightly feared the consequences of speaking my mind. Those were the days when kids actually feared their parents!

I grew up close to extended family. My uncle, aunt, and three cousins lived in the same neighborhood right around the corner from our house. Weekends consisted of family cookouts with my uncle, aunt, and their kids. We would either be at their house or they would be at ours. When we weren't in school, my cousin and I rode our bikes all over the neighborhood and through fields of what is now an industrial park. Leaving our homes right after school, we often arrived home just before dark. The little convenience store located near the entrance of the neighborhood was our desired destination for 1-cent Bazooka bubble gum and candy cigarettes. Those were the days! Life seemed much simpler then. We didn't have constant contact via cell phones, yet we survived! Can you imagine allowing our children the independence and freedom to be gone until the streetlights came on? Imagine, if you will, not having instant contact with our children and loved ones through cell phones at any given time. Yeah, neither can I.

Family traditions could always be counted on to take place year after year. We spent all birthdays at my great-grandparents' home, which was only two blocks away from our home. My great-grandparents, Granny and Grandpa, would always give me a $2 bill for my birthday; they gave all the great-grandkids a $2 bill for their birthdays. They had experienced the Great Depression, so they thought $2 was very generous. In addition to birthdays, we spent all holidays at their home, as well. On the 4th of July, my sisters and I lit Black Cats, usually during the day; my dad, being conservative with his money, wouldn't buy any of the cool firecrackers like my cousins had. When evenings arrived, the men would light the fireworks while the rest of the family watched.

Thanksgiving was another holiday spent at Granny and Grandpa's. After eating a delicious meal prepared by Granny, the men would fall asleep while the kids would play outside if the weather permitted or inside in the large back room with toys and games when the weather did not. Before going home for the evening, we'd all have dessert, returning the next day to do it all again. That same weekend, we would put up all the Christmas decorations.

Christmas Eve, we would open our one Christmas Eve gift which was *always* pajamas. I remember saying sarcastically, "Oh, I wonder what this is!" Of course, I knew exactly what it was. Although I didn't enjoy the tradition as a child, I now love the pajama tradition and plan to continue it for generations! Christmas Day after opening gifts, we again went to Granny and Grandpa's house for more gifts and dinner. Afterwards, just like Thanksgiving, all the men would fall asleep in the living room while watching television.

One of my favorite traditions included taking our annual family trip to California during spring break to visit my mom's family. We stayed all week at my grandparents' home. That week, my mom's brothers and sisters and their children came over as well. The adults stayed up all night talking and laughing and keeping the kids awake! If you've been around a traditional Hispanic family, you know how loud we can be! I loved it though. There was always so much love in my grandparents' home.

At the very young age of five, I remember being led to attend church. The bus from the neighborhood Baptist church picked up children throughout the community. I remember getting dressed and standing outside while my mom watched until the church bus came to take me to Sunday school. Oh, how I loved singing and learning and doing fun craft projects! I vividly remember a particular project. My picture was taken one week. The next week, we glued our pictures to a piece of carved wood and finished the project with a coat of lacquer. I was so proud to take it home to my parents!

When I was 11, I attended church with a friend of mine. I can't remember the exact denomination, but I remember having an amazing spiritual experience. I invited God into my life and from that point forward, I craved a more personal relationship with God. At times throughout my life, I have drifted away from my Christian walk, but I have always returned to Him.

My teen years were relatively easy considering what teens have to go through these days. My parents provided a very loving, stable home where all my needs were met and then some. Lessons my parents taught included teaching me to be responsible for my own bills by making me pay for my car insurance and fuel. I worked hard to pay for those expenses. I also paid for the things I *wanted* such as going out to eat or movies with friends. Having a job and making my own money gave me a sense of independence that I truly embraced.

I loved high school and was quite social. I was involved in many extracurricular activities including student council, cheerleading, Fellowship of Christian Athletes, baseball (stat keeper), Future Business Leaders of America, yearbook, and Spanish Club. I was voted class secretary and appointed yearbook editor. Driven in everything except math, I despise math, I excelled at school.

Relationships with my friends were very meaningful to me, and I still maintain some of those friendships today. During the weekends, I was always doing something with my friends, and even sometimes during the week. Like many other high school students, I fell in love. His name was Preston, and he was two years my senior. I was so in love; I thought I would marry him someday. Preston was a good boyfriend. No, he was a *great* boyfriend! He was gentle, kind, and patient and was not quick to anger. He loved me, and he treated me incredibly well. He enjoyed laughing and joking with our families and friends. He was definitely one of the favorites among our peers at school.

Being around Preston was easy. Even working at our relationship wasn't hard. Of course, how hard can a relationship be in high school? It's not like we had the usual stressors such as a career, rent to pay, car payments, utilities, and groceries. I'm merely comparing our relationship to the volatile ones of our peers I witnessed in which couples argued continuously. In some relationships I witnessed, one party or both were jealous and controlling. Some couples would fight, and sometimes those fights became physical. (I never actually saw the physical fights, but heard about them.)

Preston and I were very happy and content, compared to those relationships. But one day, something changed, and I became not so content. I wanted more. I didn't know what "more" meant yet. I just knew I wanted more.

2 DATING

By this time in my life, I have graduated from high school and have begun college. I'm single and loving it. Tulsa is a great city in which to be single! My good friend, Kristan, and I spend many hours just hanging out. We are inseparable! We frequent several places, but The Brink and The Full Moon are our two faves. We live to party and go out every night except Mondays and Wednesdays, the two days we catch up with the world and attend class. And yes, we do have jobs. We actually both work full-time, Monday through Friday, 8 a.m. to 5 p.m., and we both attend college in the evenings. At work we are professionals, at college we do enough to get by, and then live it up in the evenings and on the weekends! Crazy schedule, but we are young and resilient, as well as perhaps just a little dumb and naïve.

Kristan and I are outgoing and adventurous! We take weekend road trips to Oklahoma City and as far as Deep Ellum in Dallas to see the bands we love perform at various venues. We've made friends on our road trips and those friends keep us coming back, even just for a visit to them! It's always a great time! Great music! Good friends! And good drinks!

On our road trips or even just driving around town, we absolutely must have our favorite tunes. We roll the windows down, crank up the volume, and sing until we're hoarse! Every song we sing reminds us of a particular person or experience. Singing at the top of our lungs with emotions, while recalling our past experiences is exhilarating and freeing! It's like we're Thelma and Louise, however we're not running from anything… except maybe from growing up. What other time in our life will we be able to be as carefree as this? Never! This is why we're taking advantage of the moment and living it up now!

Kristan and I get free stuff everywhere we go. I don't know how we do it! It just happens! We go out to eat and get our sodas for free. Sometimes we get free desserts. Sometimes we even get our entire meals for free. Bartenders often even give us our drinks for free. It's the craziest thing! On occasions, guys try to buy us drinks, which I most often decline. I don't *need* a guy to buy me a drink, and I definitely don't want to lead a guy on by allowing him to buy me a drink. On the very rare occasion we allow guys to buy us drinks, we go to the bar with them, place the order with the bartender, and get our drink directly from the bartender. We are too scared of the date rape drug, so we play it smart. Life is great!

You may be wondering by now when we have time to date. The truth is dating isn't a high priority on our list. But when we do date, we typically go on double dates. Since we usually meet guys in pairs, there is a guy for her to date and a guy for me to date. Typically after an outing or two, we find something we don't like about them. So, we kindly, or rather rudely, stop returning their phone calls and go on with our life. If I have any advice to give at this point, it would be to gently inform people when you no longer want to date them. It is the worst experience to run into them later in life and either act as though you don't know each other although it is obvious you both do, or you actually have to speak to them. Either way, it's not a good situation, and it is incredibly awkward and uncomfortable for everyone. Yes, I've experienced both.

Because Kristan and I are regulars at The Brink, we develop relationships with others who are also regulars. It is like a little community of regulars. We have developed friendships with one of the local Tulsa bands, so much so that we go with them to some of their out of town concerts. Some called us roadies. But we are more than that; we are friends!

Kristan and I have fake names that we give when people meet us out and about. Although we love to party, we are smart, or at least we think we are smart about it. I am Mary – from a nickname my dad often calls me, Lisa Mary, which was derived from my real name, Lisa Marie. It's the first name that popped in my head one day when asked for my name by some creepo I didn't want to talk to... and it's an easy name for me to remember!

It's a random Sunday night at The Brink. My friend and I are sitting along the edge of the dance floor. Some random guy in a white sweater is standing behind us... alone. After standing there for about five minutes, he finally walks off. I ask Kristan, "Who was that weirdo? What an idiot standing there by himself!" Really, there are only maybe 10 people in the entire place. It is still early... around 9 p.m. The crowd doesn't typically come out until after 10 p.m. or 11 p.m.

My friend and I decide to leave a little after midnight. As we start walking to the front door, white sweater man approaches me. He asks for my name and for some unknown reason, without hesitation, I reply, "Lisa." He tells me his is Lon. He then asks questions only a very observant person would ask such as, "Didn't you used to have long hair?" I reply, "Yes." He asks, "And was it curly?" I reply, "Yes." He states as a question, "And you had highlights?" I reply, "Yes." It's been about a month since I got my hair cut into a Princess Di style, which is a popular style at the moment. To get this new do, I had to cut off my curls and highlights. Needless to say, I am a little shocked but intrigued that this random guy remembers so much about me.

So what do I do? I give him my number... my actual cell phone number. I give him my number without even thinking twice about it... without even thinking once about it! I suppose I am not only intrigued by this guy, but I'm impressed with his attractive appearance - short dark hair, smooth face free of facial hair, straight white teeth, great smile, blue eyes, muscular yet lean, and somewhat shy but risk-taking demeanor. I am anxious to see where this leads.

Over the next few weeks, white sweater guy and I talk on the phone multiple times. Well, we mostly sit on the phone together while he talks to his friends who are with him at his home. Of course, I'm much more mature than this junior-high-acting-person who lacks social skills with the opposite sex, so I end these phone conversations after about 10 minutes of this nonsense. Yet I still answer the phone when he calls again. I suppose I answer because of my curiosity about him. He's mysterious and doesn't really let me get to know him. Yet he calls me; he pursues me. And a girl likes being pursued.

During a phone conversation, Lon asks me to meet him out at the Brink, the place we met, to hang out one night. Of course I want to go although he's not a very good conversationalist. His attractiveness makes up for his lack of communication abilities.

Like any girl who is going out to meet a cute guy, I spend extra time getting ready to look my best. And of course, I have a sidekick! My friend, Kristan, and I do everything together! Meeting Lon at the Brink is no exception!

When we get there, I'm feeling really excited to see him. We walk in the door and as soon as my eyes adjust to the darkness, my eyes find him. He looks great, of course. Handsome, clean cut, with a trim physique. I walk over to him, and we greet each other. He doesn't say anything about how nice I look, but his expressions and half-smiles say enough. We decide to get a table on the edge of the dance floor. As we walk towards the tables, he takes my hand and leads the way. I like that he takes the lead and guides me. I think it shows strength. At this point and less than 10 minutes into our outing, I'm a little giddy. I haven't felt this way in a while.

Shortly after we sit at the table, the band comes out on stage and starts playing. Lon puts his arm around the back of my chair and essentially around me. Kristan and I get up to dance a few times; we love to dance! And every time I come back to my seat, Lon again puts his arm around the back of my chair. Towards the end of the night, we all get up from the table and stand in a circle talking to each other. Lon, during this time, has his arm around the bottom of my back with his hand resting on my side opposite of him. This is not acceptable to me. He does not know me well enough place his arm around me in this manner. I am a little turned off at this point. No, I'm really turned off at this point!

Lon and his friend decide to leave, and he asks me to walk him to the front door. I am not impressed that he's leaving, but I choose to walk him to the door anyway. As we get close to the door, Lon turns to me and asks for a kiss goodbye. I tell him that I don't kiss in public, and I don't believe in PDA (public display of affection). I think he's a little shocked at my prudeness, but respects it and leaves.

At this point, I decide I won't ever go out with him again!

3 TURN OF EVENTS

Life was going well; I had just started my new job about 4 months ago. I was recruited away from my stable recruiting job at WorldCom to work for an IT recruiting firm, accepting their position of Professional Development Manager. Basically, I am the liaison between our employees in the field, our client companies, and our internal management at our branch. I love this job! I get to take employees to lunch every day, and it is my responsibility to visit each employee at least once per month to continue to develop and foster a relationship with them so that they feel valued and truly a part of our company.

It's a Monday, and I am brought into my manager's office. I get the news. The company is downsizing per a directive from corporate in Chicago. All offices have to be uniform – same number of Recruiters, Sales Reps, Professional Development Managers, etc. Our office already had a Professional Development Manager before hiring me. Since I'm the newest employee hired, I am the first to be laid off. I've never been through a layoff. I have no idea how to feel except maybe a little numb. I go home and start updating my resume.

The next morning, I am slow getting up and around. Around noon, my sister and her husband come over. I greet them and we start to chat. And then I realize… It's Tuesday. Why are they at my house? They both have jobs and work during regular business hours Monday through Friday. They should be at work right now. That is when I become aware, they both have a look of dismay on their face. And then they tell me... My uncle died earlier this morning. He had been sick for some time, but he's only 45. Who saw this coming? Maybe it was inevitable, but I never even thought about the consequences of his illness before today. But now, I have to think about it. I have to process it. Immediately, I begin to feel saddened, but not just for me. I feel saddened for my dad. He had lost one of his brothers a little less than 20 years ago. And now he has lost his other brother. I ache for my cousins. They no longer have a dad. I ache for my Granny and Grandpa. They shouldn't have to bury yet another grandson. And so the grieving process begins.

*****

I think one thing that adds a different dynamic to the grieving process is that my uncle and my dad have worked together at the same company for over 25 years. They have some incredible people with whom they have worked, many of which are here at the funeral. The support and respect for my uncle, my dad, and my uncle's family from these co-workers is overwhelming.

In my family, I have often been labeled as the "strong one." And because I'm that strong one, I find myself sitting between my two sisters, each with their heads on my shoulders. My arms are around them, comforting them as they cry. Although my parents are sitting on the row in front of me, I can still see their pain. I see the pain in my cousins and my aunt. I see the pain in my Granny and Grandpa. My heart is broken for everyone. But I refuse to cry. I'm a private person and prefer to grieve alone. Besides, I know when I start crying, it's explosive and ugly. I don't want to ugly cry here.

And then it happens. I start laughing. Yes, I actually start laughing at my beloved uncle's funeral. As inappropriate as it is, it's happening. It's involuntary, a nervous reaction. I'm trying to keep myself from crying and the result is laughter. Nothing is funny. There is absolutely nothing funny about this. As I recognize how sick and twisted this may seem to others, I finally give myself permission to cry and allow myself to grieve in front of all these people. I realize I can still be strong for my sisters even as I cry. And so, my laughter turns to tears.

It's the evening after my uncle's funeral. All the family gathers at my parents' home to celebrate my uncle's life. After being with them for about an hour, I decide to meet up with my good friend, John. At this point, he is my only support system outside of my family. In the interim, Kristan has become really serious with a guy, and I don't want to burden her with my sadness right now. John is gentle and has a very kind heart. And he's interested in me. Unfortunately, the feeling is not mutual. I have tried to make it mutual, but it just isn't happening.

John and I meet at the Full Moon, one of our favorite places to hang out. We just relax and visit, talking about the funeral. I mention my uncle's name, Larry. And John says, "Hi. My name is Darrell. This is my brother Larry and my other brother Larry." (A reference to an 80's sitcom, Newhart.) After laughing hysterically, I tell John that my dad's name is actually Deryl. Yes, it's true. My dad's name is Deryl, and his brother's name was Larry. Weird coincidence but John feels terrible at this point. However, I am laughing so hard, partially because John is so mortified and apologetic and partially because it's so silly that it's funny. This is the first time that I've laughed – really laughed – since my uncle passed. And it feels good.

My friend, John, plays in a local band that is absolutely loved by Tulsans. As previously mentioned, this is the band whose members Kristan I have befriended. It's about a week after my uncle's passing, and I'm at the Brink (my absolute favorite place) watching John and his band. Guess who I see… Lon. He has been calling me off and on for a few months, but I never return his calls. I try to stay hidden because I don't want to acknowledge that I've purposely been ignoring him. I hate confrontation, so I avoid it at all costs.

I'm on my way to the bathroom and coming towards me is Lon. I think to myself, "If I don't make eye contact, he won't see me."

Wrong! He lightly touches my arm to get my attention. I stop and acknowledge his presence, and with my facial expression and with an incredible attitude ask, "What do you want?" without even saying a word. He tells me he's been trying to call me. I explain that I haven't wanted to talk to him. I tell him it's all because he put his arm around me the last time we went out a few months ago, and I'm not interested in that. I tell him that he doesn't know me well enough to display that kind of affection. He doesn't know me that well period, and that was our first date. I again reiterate that I just don't like that sort of thing and stomped off to the bathroom. Uncomfortable moment!

I go back to my table and watch the band play. They are awesome! I LOVE listening to them! They sing a song referring to a girl with brown eyes. However, they change the lyrics to reference green eyes instead of brown because I have green eyes. Seriously! Yes, cheesy, I know! This goes back to the issue of John liking me in a different way than I like him. But the sentiment is nice, I must admit. John is such a nice guy. Why can't I just like him?

Towards the end of the evening, I see someone approaching my table out of the corner of my eye. I cannot believe this! It's Lon. Can't he get a clue? He walks right up to me and asks, "If I promise not to touch you, can we go out on a date?" Before I had a chance to process his question, the word, "Yes," comes right out of my mouth. Have I lost my mind? Maybe. But when I really think about it, the truth is, I have nothing better to do. So, why not? He knows where I stand with the PDA subject. At least that's out of the way!

The weekend rolls around, and Lon and I have made plans to meet at Bennigan's, a little Irish pub and restaurant. Initially, we were to meet at 7 p.m. At 6:30 p.m, I receive a call from Lon asking if we can push it back 30 minutes because he's not yet ready. Truth be told, I was ready by 5 p.m.; I was excited and a little anxious and ready to go. Why was I so excited and anxious? Maybe it was Lon's mysterious ways that intrigued me. As disappointed as I was to wait 30 more minutes, I waited.

Then, I got another call from Lon, pushing back the meeting time by 30 more minutes. Believe it or not, I received 2 more calls delaying our meeting time by 30 minutes each time. What does a guy have to do to get ready? How much primping must he do? His hair is super short, so I know it's not his hair. I'm baffled. But whatever, I have nothing better to do, right?

Finally, at 9 p.m., we meet at Bennigan's. Yes, we meet at the restaurant rather than having him pick me up. I'm not a pick-me-up-for-a-date kind of girl. I like my independence, and I like people not knowing where I live! When Lon and I approached each other, I determine from the looks and smell of Lon, it was worth the wait. My, does he look good! He is handsome! His skin is flawless. Great smile with white, straight teeth. His eyes have an interesting yet attractive almond shape; very nice and warm to look into. He's wearing a sweater that slightly shows his thick biceps and chest muscles. Soft eyes and face yet strong physique. I think I might be able to make it through this dinner – and not just make it through but actually enjoy it.

Our conversation is very relaxed and free flowing. Lon is easy to talk to but a man of few words. We have some similarities including our taste in music. We both are middle children and have sisters. And, he seems to adore his mom! I believe that the way a man treats his mom is an indication of how he will treat his girlfriend or wife. I'm glad to know he respects and admires his mom. He has goals and plans for his career. I appreciate that he has those outlined. In addition to our similarities, we also have some differences. He has a passion for fast cars and car stereos. I just care that I have a car and music in it! But our differences are what make the world go round, right?

Although this could have been true, I will shortly be proven otherwise...

4 MARRIAGE

Lon and I see each other often – several times a week. We laugh quite a bit. He's easy to talk to. He always smells amazing! And he always looks so attractive! My phone conversations with Lon could be a little better. He is not very talkative on the phone, and quite honestly, it's not much different in person. He's simply a man of few words. His friends are great, and they all seem very respectful. They are accepting and welcoming to me. I enjoy hanging out with them all.

On my lunch break, I occasionally take sweet hand-written notes and put them on Lon's car when he's at work. He seems to appreciate those. Just driving up to his work gives me butterflies – I'm excited to leave him the note, excited to know he's going to read it and know that I was thinking of him, and nervous about getting caught hoping he doesn't see me!

Months go by. We are dating exclusively and really seem to be good together. And then it happens... I realize I'm a few days late on my period. Yes, I had premarital sex. This is not something I am proud of but yes, it was something I did. And without even taking a pregnancy test, I just know that I'm pregnant. My intuition is telling me I am pregnant.

I call an office that offers pregnancy testing and they are able to get me in after lunch. So I drink lots and lots and lots of water so that I can be fully ready to take the pregnancy test. By the time I get to their office, I am about to urinate all over myself. I run in and am greeted by two precious older ladies. They are just so sweet… and a little slow considering how my bladder is about to force some of the liquid out of my body! I complete the required documentation, and run into their restroom. I place the pregnancy test on the top of the toilet paper roll, sit down on the toilet, and completely empty my bladder. Ahhhh, such relief! I am so thankful that I made it to the restroom without having an accident all over myself! And then I realize the pregnancy test is still sitting on top of the toilet paper roll. I cannot believe this! So, I stand up and jump up and down as if this is going to help get more of the water I consumed through my system faster. Oh, and did I mention that this office closes in 10 minutes?

I sit back down in total disbelief! I went through the last 4 -5 hours of drinking a ton of water and depriving my body the opportunity to eliminate the fluids! Thankfully about 3 minutes later, I feel as though I might be able to urinate again. And, this time I do so using the pregnancy test! I quickly wash my hands and take my pregnancy test to the front desk, not even taking a peek at the results. I'm in a hurry because I know they're closing in a few moments. The sweet little ladies at the front desk congratulate me on the little bundle of joy I am now expecting, confirming what my intuition had already told me. They ask me if the dad knows yet. I advise that he does not, but definitely would later tonight.

I am still not in freak-out mode. I've been calmly saying to myself, "Well, this is what is happening. We can do this. We are going to do this." By saying "we," I'm referring to myself and this baby. At this point, I don't even know how Lon is going to react. We've talked about children and I know at some point, he wants a girl. But I'm also sure that "at some point" does not mean right now. Sometimes life throws us some curve balls, and most often those curve balls are a result of our own choices. I own this choice. I own the decisions I made that got me here. And we're going to be ok.

I call Lon to schedule a time for the two of us to get together tonight. I say the words men hate, "We need to talk." I suggest we go to a public, somewhat louder establishment, as I am unsure as to how he will react. If we go to a loud place, no one will really be able to hear our conversation, nor his reaction.

So we meet. And I explain, "I missed my period. And the reason for that is I'm pregnant." I explain that I went to a professional testing location that confirmed my suspicions with a pregnancy test. He sits there for a moment and then asks, "Are you sure? Are they sure they're sure?" And then he asks again, "Are you sure? Are you sure they're sure?" Of course I'm sure. I may joke a lot, but this is no joking matter.

We discuss our options. I advise him that I'm having this baby, and I don't need him to be a part of the process if that's what he chooses. I also explain that he can simply walk away at this very moment, and he will never hear from me again. Before leaving that evening, however, we choose to have this baby... together.

Lon is involved in all of my doctor's appointments. He goes with me to the ultrasound where we learn we are going to have a baby girl. Each day, we become more excited and at the same time a little more nervous. We have no idea what to expect, but we are sharing in the experiences of each new day. He's helpful and still very respectful. He's gentle and kind and accommodating. He's involved and very sweet. I am certain he's going to make an amazing dad.

I am now 7 ½ months pregnant. Lon enjoys being with his dad and spends as much time as he can with him. One evening, we go out to dinner with Lon's dad. Afterwards, Lon and his dad play a few games of pool. On our way home, we are driving about 45 miles per hour when a car turns right in front of us. It is inevitable; we t-bone the car. Lon's head hits the windshield; he's not wearing a seatbelt. However, he walks away with only a headache. Thankfully, I am wearing my seatbelt and have only a burn on my neck from the seatbelt. The teenage driver of the other car who has a suspended license is fine and injury-free. I am thankful that we are alright but little do I know that this is the beginning of a long, drawn out end.

Our much anticipated baby girl is born in December. Lon is fabulous throughout the entire labor and delivery as are his mom and my mom. He has been very supportive and patient all the while he's been scared and nervous! Lon chooses to name our little girl Ashlyn Bree. Ashlyn means "dream" and "vision." Bree means "strong" and "honorable." Beautiful, precious name! And it's more fitting than I could have ever known.

Ashlyn is a sweet, relaxed baby. She projectile vomits (spits up) on everything after every feeding, but is as happy as she can be. She smiles all the time. She smiles when she hears my voice even if she can't see me. She smiles at anyone who looks at her or talks to her. She smiles when she sees a familiar face. She is so amazing and has enriched our lives.

Lon and I decide to make our family official and we get married when Ashlyn is 5 months old. A month after we get married, I find out Lon is addicted to pain medication as a result of the car accident we had 7 ½ months ago. Lon and I discuss the problem, and he promises to stop taking the medication. I'm relieved and thankful.

A few months go by when I begin to notice money missing from our bank account. I also realize Lon is no longer affectionate. He is becoming more distant with me and even more quiet. And he is beginning to make excuses not to attend family functions. That is when I discover his addiction to pain medication has worsened. His doctor is a family friend who continues to increase his prescription of hydrocodone and has even called in his prescription to seven different pharmacies so that Lon can get a 1-month supply from *each* of the seven pharmacies *each* month. I talk to Lon about it. He swears he doesn't have a problem and can stop at any time. However, he doesn't stop.

Right after Ashlyn's 1st birthday, I find out I'm pregnant again. I inform Lon. I use the word "inform" because that's where we are at this point. We don't actually communicate much. I'm the adult in the relationship with every aspect of our lives, as he continues to regress due to his drug addiction. After informing Lon, I break down and cry. I am sobbing for about 4 hours, not because of the pregnancy per se, but because my world is crumbling down around me. I have no control or ability to change things, and I'm bringing yet another life into this mess. After my four-hour crying session, I make the choice to pull up my big-girl panties and move forward.

5 THE BEGINNING OF THE END

It is Friday night about 8 p.m. on Easter weekend. I am 5 months pregnant. Ashlyn is 16 months old, sick with a fever and has been vomiting. Lon decides that he needs to go to his friend's house to retrieve some pants that his friend recently borrowed. So, Lon takes a shower, shaves, puts some gel in his hair, applies quite a bit of cologne, and gets dressed in clothes that are nicer than any that you would wear to a friend's house just to pick up a pair of pants. I'm not buying it. I request that Lon stay at home tonight and get his pants tomorrow, as Ashlyn is ill and if I need to run to the store or if she gets worse and needs to go to the emergency room, I'd really like for him to be here to help. He blatantly refuses my request.

Shortly after Lon leaves, I decide to get Ashlyn up and drive over to Lon's friend's house. As I suspected, Lon isn't there. I begin to feel anxious. Lon is continuously full of lies these days. I think he would even say the sky is green just for the sake of lying. At this point, I'm at a loss as to where he is, but I realize I might have an idea. There is a bar in Tulsa that his dad frequents regularly. His dad introduced Lon to the bar years ago and when the two of them want to hang out, this is often the place they go. It's cute and quaint and somewhat classy for a bar. So, I drive to this place and just as I anticipated, I see Lon's car. Whew! At least I know where he is! And I see Lon's dad's truck. Awesome! They are both here. I think to myself, "Nothing bad can possibly happen since his dad is here." I decide to go back home and put Ashlyn back to bed since she is ill. Home is really where I should have been anyway, but my curiosity and anxiety got the best of me.

It's 2 a.m. and Lon still isn't home, so I'm pacing the floor. I haven't had a wink of sleep. I'm exhausted, worried, and have thought of every possibility under the stars at this point. Is he still on pills? Did he get into a wreck? Did he get arrested for a DUI? Did he go home with someone? Another hour goes by. It's 3 a.m., and Lon finally stumbles in. I ask him where he's been all night, and he basically tells me that he was spending time with his dad. He also says that he doesn't have to tell me anything, and that I'm just a stupid bitch. He goes upstairs and goes to bed.

I'm crushed. I stayed up, sacrificed sleep, worried about his safety all for this? To be told that I'm not even important enough for him to provide me with an explanation of his whereabouts this evening while I stayed home, pregnant and taking care of our sick 16 month old daughter. I sit on the couch and cry as I wonder when this nightmare is going to end. I'm certainly not a priority in his life. And as he continues down this drug-addicted road, I become less and less important to him, almost as though I'm not even a person anymore. But I am a good wife. I work and bring home as much (if not more) money than he does. I ensure the bills get paid. I handle the grocery shopping and I cook. I care for our daughter. Also, I take care of myself; I try to look attractive everyday. Most importantly, I take care of our family.

Is this the reality of marriage? Is this what marriage is all about? This is definitely not how I envisioned my adult life to be. This is not what I dreamed of for my life. This is absolutely not how I see things transpire in all the chick flicks I have watched. What has happened to my life?

*****

I can't go to sleep. My mind keeps racing. I am trying to determine where I fit in Lon's order of importance so I make a list.

Here's what I've come up with:

1) Pills
2) His car
3) His dad
4) His friends
5) His job
6) His mom
7) His sisters
8) Our daughter
9) Food
10) TV
11) Sleep
12) Me

Now, this isn't a poor-pitiful-me session, nor is it a pity party. I truly am trying to determine where I fit into his life and determine how I became such a low priority on the list. I'm analytical and very solution focused. If I can figure this out, then maybe I can do something to move higher on his list of priorities and importance. Somehow, some way, this will all be resolved. I'm determined to change my standing and fix this situation.

Being determined to have a loving, lasting, and fulfilling marriage requires incredible strength for me specifically when Lon says ugly, hurtful things. He often tells me things like, "You're stupid! You're the reason I do drugs because you're such a bitch! I can't stand you!" It's hard to hear those words. I choose to ignore the ugliness, swallow my pride, and pray he gets clean.

If I'm really honest with myself, then I begin to see how I have changed. No longer am I the carefree, easygoing girl I once was. I am no longer patient. I no longer have fun. I no longer laugh. I don't like who I've become. As the situation worsens, I find myself looking through his things... looking for pills. He spends more money than he earns to pay for his drug addiction. Considering his spending is so out of control, I know that somewhere there are pills to find. I look through his car including the console, under the seats, in the glove box, and even behind the glove box. I search the kitchen cabinets and drawers. I look in the pockets of all of his pants. I look in his dresser drawers and in the closet. I search his toiletries. I even look in the couch cushions. Previously, I've found pill bottles hidden in all of those places. My every thought, throughout the day, is consumed with him and his drug addiction. The financial stress of him spending the money he earns plus some of mine creates even more frustration!

For the past few months, Lon has continued to communicate that he's no longer using pills. Because his behavior contradicts his claim, I don't believe he is being honest. He lies regularly about his whereabouts. He lies about the things on which he is spending our money or rather he denies spending money at all. Our bank account is proof that he's not being honest. So I decide to get the truth on my own. I purchased some recording equipment to "tap" our home phone to see if he has phone conversations regarding drugs. I am desperate for answers. While he was gone last night, I set it up. This is before cell phone use was so prevalent. We shall see what information is gathered from this detective work.

He's hung over today, not surprisingly. It's Easter. He'll spend all day recovering from "hanging with his dad" while I spend the day with my parents, sisters, and their families. I'll make an excuse, like I always do, that he's not feeling well and because he's not feeling well, he's not participating in our family functions. I won't communicate to my family the truth – that he's a drug addict. Why don't I tell them? I don't want them to know. I don't want them to judge him. I don't want them to judge me for staying. I'll carry on with a smile on my face, trying to look as peaceful as possible hoping that no one sees my broken heart or my hopelessness.

After a great day with Ashlyn and my family, I return home to find Lon lying on the couch still not feeling 100%. I make an excuse to run to the store just so that I can get out of the house and hear the day's phone recordings. I sneak the tape and portable tape player out of the house, drive to a nearby store parking lot, and began to

24

listen to the tape. Much to my surprise, there were about a total of 2 hours of phone conversations on that tape. That's a lot of talking, especially for Lon.

Of course, he speaks negatively about me. He calls me ugly names to others. No surprise there. And although it's no surprise, it still stings a little hearing those words come out of his mouth... Hearing him slam me, the one person who he committed to sharing life with, raising children with, who takes care of his household, who loves him, and who continues fighting for this marriage. Unfortunately, I am the only one fighting for this marriage.

I continue to listen to the recordings. And then I hear it. I hear the truth about last night. He's talking to his friend while his friend is having dinner with his wife. Lon tells his friend that after his friend left last night, he continued to stay at the bar. He said, "I started f&^%ing around with Michelle. She has some really nice tits." His friend responded, while having dinner with his wife, "Well, was it any good?"

Was it any good?!?!?!? This man should be telling his friend that he needs to get his butt home to his wife instead of being at the bar! This man should communicate to his friend that his self-destructive decisions are going to cost him his family. This man should expect more for his friend and out of his friend. But his response to Lon's statements about cheating on me, his wife, was, "Well, was it any good?" Really?!?!?

I am devastated. I thought I was going to hear recordings about pills, not infidelity. I even know this girl, Michelle. She is a bartender there and has been for several years. She knows who I am. She also knows that Lon is married. She is aware that Lon has a daughter and another one on the way. What's worse is that she has absolutely no class, nor does she exhibit self-respect in the way she dresses or in her interactions with others. This is the kind of girl with whom Lon would rather be?!? My whole world is crumbling right here, this moment, in my car in a store parking lot. I know this is the beginning of the end. I know he isn't going to change. I also know he is continuing to go downhill, and I refuse to let him take me with him, to be a victim of his choices. I deserve better than this. I have to take immediate action.

(For the record, Michelle has no breasts. Just saying.)

6 SINGLE MOTHERHOOD

I return home from listening to the recordings of Lon's evening. I want to discuss this with Lon and what better way to start the conversation than to let him listen to his own words coming out of his own mouth! Brutal? Maybe. But I'm willing and ready to do it! I want to see his reaction. Basically, I want him to see me hearing his disgusting words. I want him to know I heard him loud and clear. And, I'm ready for whatever may transpire as a result. Of course, I have another copy of the tape, as I went to my parents' house to make a copy. The proof is essential; I want to ensure I keep the proof. And yes, I had just given my parents a 5-minute summary of the last year of Lon's continuing and worsening addiction to prescription medication and the fact that I was finished fighting for this marriage – last night was the last straw.

I go inside our home and sit on the couch carrying my portable tape player with me. I ask Lon to sit on the couch because I have something I want him to hear. He obliges. I push play and we both hear his voice say the words, "I had a really great time last night. I started f&^%ing around with Michelle. She has some really nice tits." As soon as he starts hearing his own voice, he looks down at the ground. He knows he is busted. During the second sentence, he stands to his feet, not saying a word. After the third sentence, I turn off the tape player. Lon's first words to me are, "Our marriage was

27

over before it even began." So I ask him why he even married me. He doesn't answer. Nothing matters at this moment except moving on with my life with some sort of dignity.

I tell Lon I am going to move out by next weekend and that I'm taking Ashlyn with me. I explain that we can work out the details for visitation with Ashlyn later. Thank goodness he has a business trip for which he has to leave tomorrow and will not return until next weekend. I know I can't handle being around him right now, seeing his face, knowing that our family isn't enough for him, knowing that I'm not enough for him, knowing he would rather have someone else, and knowing the person he chose last night was someone so revolting and repulsive.

Tomorrow is Monday and somehow I have to get some rest so that I can get up tomorrow, put on my happy face, go to work, and carry on as though all is well. I've had a lot of practice at this over the past year, but never with these particular circumstances. I am determined to get through this.

*****

I get through the work week, thank God! I'm able to secure a two-bedroom apartment in Broken Arrow with a move in date of Saturday. With the help of my parents, sisters, and their husbands, we have a moving crew that gets my stuff packed and loaded that Saturday. Shortly before we leave my house, Lon shows up. He looks shocked and confused. I'm not sure why. Perhaps he just didn't think I was serious when I said I was going to move out. But the truth is, I am moving out, and that day is today.

I am getting settled in my new apartment. It's brand new. New carpet. New everything. It even smells new. If my marriage is ending and I have to move, this is definitely the place to go! It helps me feel better about my fresh start.

Ashlyn is adjusting well. Every now and then she goes to the window, looks out, and while shrugging her shoulders and extending her arms slightly with palms facing up asks, "Daddy?" I simply respond, "Daddy's bye-bye." Because she is only 16 months old, she has no concept of time. She doesn't realize, as the weeks go by, that she hasn't seen her dad in weeks... even months

May, June, and July go by and it's now August. Ashlyn has seen her dad fewer times than I can count on one hand. He hasn't paid one penny to help me with childcare or food or even to get ready for our second child who is expected to grace us with her presence this month. I've had a few false alarms where I've gone to the hospital and on the way, have called Lon to notify him in case he wants to be there. Each time I've called, he hasn't answered his cell phone. So, I've called his office. Each time I've called the office, his boss has told me that Lon was with me at the hospital. Well, I knew better because I wasn't even at the hospital – I was *on my way* to the hospital, and Lon didn't even know yet! The truth is, he is using me as an excuse to leave work to go get more pills to maintain his high. Lon's addiction is worsening. When is he going to hit rock bottom?

The day has finally come. I woke up to discover that I'm in labor. Immediately, I call my mom for help. Thank goodness she only lives 2 miles away! She rushes over and helps me get Ashlyn ready. We drop Ashlyn off at childcare and are on our way to the hospital. I call Lon and notify him that this is the real deal, and he tells me he has to go to work today and will see if he can leave early. Time goes by. I'm having horrific back labor. I'm angry I'm doing this without him. He's part of the reason I'm here in this current state! I call him around noon and give him an earful, telling him he should be here rubbing my back. He tells me that his boss won't let him leave. Lon has used my pregnancy as an excuse to leave work too much – although it was *never* the reason he left work. He has abused his boss' trust so that at this moment, his boss doesn't believe anything he says.

My labor and delivery support system include my mom and longtime friend, Jessica. My dad is there as well, but definitely not for assistance! Shortly before 6 p.m., Alayna is born. My mom and Jess are present to share in the miracle of this birth. I will be forever grateful for them, as I feel alone in this process of having a baby with someone who doesn't make his own children a priority, not even the birth of his second child. When I finally get to see Alayna, I think, "Oh my goodness! She looks just like her dad! I love her anyway!"

Over the next year, our divorce is finalized. Visitation and child support are outlined, neither of which is followed. Lon definitely doesn't pay one red cent for anything. In fact, on a regular basis, he tells me he isn't going to give me *any* money. He comes over occasionally to pick Ashlyn up for an afternoon but never exercises his full visitation. Also, he never chooses to have visitation with Alayna because she's a baby and is too much responsibility. Well, as the only participating parent of two parents, *I* don't get the option of picking and choosing when I take care of my kids and when I don't. And *I* don't get the option of picking and choosing what financial obligations I meet and which ones I don't meet. I have to pay them all! And I have to pay them completely on my own with zero help. Childcare, formula, diapers, food, clothes… Childcare alone is over $200 each week. I should not have to pay for those expenses alone. I've even offered for him to pay only half of the childcare and nothing else, but he still won't help.

One thing I can say is that Ashlyn loves her daddy. She is always so excited to see him. And when he comes to see Ashlyn, he is really excited to see her, too. I know he loves her. Even with his issues, I know he does. But his inconsistent visits communicate that she's not a priority, and Ashlyn deserves better. Alayna definitely deserves better.

*****

Alayna is now 1. She's super cute, funny, and full of life. Ashlyn is 2 ½ and is sweet, gentle, outgoing, independent, and a little bossy with her little sister, Alayna. I just love these two girls. And Lon seems to be doing better. He is increasing his interaction with the girls. Alayna is a mommy's girl and doesn't like to go with Lon, so he comes over often to see her. I think he may be off his pills now. He seems level headed with a clear thought process. Lately, he has been very kind to me. He has also started taking better care of himself. He is even trying to help contribute financially. I'm impressed with him and his improvement.

We decide to "date" to see if we begin liking each other again. Maybe if we start liking each other again and if things go well, we can ultimately bring our family back together. We are enjoying each other's company. We're laughing together again. We're enjoying the girls together. We are eating family meals together. We are doing things together as a family. All is relaxed. All is well. Lon is even attending family gatherings with my parents and sisters. This truly is amazing! Almost miraculous! It feels really good. I feel hopeful that maybe we can make it. Maybe my girls can be raised in a home with both parents after all! I have hope for our family.

And then, bam! I realize that Lon is now abusing alcohol, and a lot of it. He has simply traded one addiction for another. He drinks alcohol at night after he leaves my apartment. He wasn't forthcoming about that. Why would he be? He's an addict. Addicts hide – or try to hide – their addictions. Once again, my hope is destroyed and my spirit is crushed.

And then yet another bam! I discover I'm pregnant. Well, if that doesn't throw me a curve ball! Ultimately I know that God plans all children. He planned Ashlyn. He planned Alayna. And He planned this unborn child I'm carrying. Knowing that this child has a purpose enables me to move forward, confident in successfully getting through this pregnancy. I've been through a pregnancy alone, and I can get through it again.

Lon goes back to using pills. He goes back to his ugly ways, calling me ugly names and blaming me and everyone else but his dad for his drug use. I work full-time while taking care of my two precious girls. Through the grace of God, I am able to meet my financial obligations while having just enough money for food and gas. God indeed does provide.

One of the most incredible ways God has provided was today. It's the 5th of the month. My rent of $495 was due on the 1st. I have a grand total of $20 in my bank account and won't be getting paid until Friday. The girls and I go to church. During the offering, I felt led to write a check for that $20. I pray to God, "God, this is my only $20. I know you're going to provide for me even if it's a homeless shelter. I trust You and know You will provide." When I return home from church, I have a message on my answering machine from Lon's mom. She said, "Lisa, I have a check for you for $500. I know it's not much, but it's all I have to give." I fall to my knees and cry out to God thanking Him. I'm in awe of Him. You see, Lon's mom works two jobs just to make ends meet for her own financial obligations. She doesn't have that kind of money to give. Somehow, she did this time. That somehow was all God's doing.

*****

During my ultrasound, I get the biggest surprise of my life. I find out I'm having a son. I cry tears of happiness as I sit there in disbelief. I'm thrilled at the news. And at that very moment, I vow to never allow my son to be like his father. I will work diligently my entire life to ensure I do not raise my son to be like Lon.

Six months go by and I give birth to Aiden. This time, Lon was there for the labor and delivery, but he was so high that he may as well have not been there. Actually, I would have preferred he wasn't there. Instead of helping me, he created a stressful environment. I was in labor for 23 hours, during which time my Granny was passing away in the same hospital just two floors up. My mom was with her but would periodically come check on me. As usual, I put on a noble façade that all was well. I had to. She needed to be with my Granny, not me.

At one point while I was in labor, I had to go to the restroom and asked Lon for help getting there. He was stumbling and slurring his speech. I was so very tired. I didn't want to deal with him. So, I asked him to go get my mom. His response was, "You're just trying to make a scene." A scene? For who? No one was around. I just wanted my mom for just a moment to make me feel better, just with her presence – not to share my frustration about Lon, but to just have her there.

Everything changed that day at noon   From the moment I laid eyes on Aiden, I knew he was angelic.   God had sent him to me. God had sent him here.   Aiden will change the family tree of the men in his family genealogy and heritage by respecting and honoring women and by truly respecting himself.   I'm determined to raise him to be the husband that I never had, one that honors his wife, his family, and God.

So here I am, a single mother of three beautiful children, all under the age of 3 ½. It is not easy, but I am incredibly blessed. Although I may not have much, I have all I need. I will do my part. God will do the rest. God indeed provides.

7 KNIGHT IN SHINING ARMOR

Aiden is now 9 months old. Alayna is 2. Ashlyn is 4. These precious beings are what gets me up each morning and what makes me pass out with exhaustion at night! They are such great kids. Everywhere we go, people always comment on how well behaved they are. Even in the grocery store, they are such angels. They never ask for anything and are calm and obedient. You should see me grocery shopping! I have two shopping carts - one full of kids with Aiden in the front in the child seat and the girls in the back, larger part of the cart. Then I have another shopping cart for the groceries. I'm sure it's quite the sight!

Although I've done quite well financially, the economy has somewhat tanked for people in my profession, IT Recruiting, so I've been forced to find employment in another industry. I now work in sales at a company that helps people with hair loss. The clients are primarily men, although we do have female clients. Most often, the clients are quite professional and friendly; perhaps it's because we interact with them when they are most vulnerable, talking about how their hair loss has negatively impacted their lives. At one point, a body builder, someone you expect to be self confident, cried because he was so devastated. He spoke about how he hated losing his hair and how devastating his hair loss was to him. I never would have imagined men felt this way prior to working here.

There's one client who comes in each week – every Thursday actually. He is not the most handsome guy ever, but his personality comes through and makes his smile a little brighter. There's something endearing about his childlike, innocent demeanor. His laugh is cute and his mannerisms are alluring. He takes care of himself; he works out and has a nice, muscular build. I love that he has kids, and he actually makes them a priority. In fact, he has lunch with his 2nd grade son every Thursday after his appointment here. I'm intrigued and impressed with this guy. Recently, I've noticed that I've been spending a little extra time getting ready each Thursday morning. I make sure I'm present in the office when he arrives and participate in the light chitchat that takes place between him and the office staff.

Others in our office have noticed the way I light up when he comes to the office and have said that although he's always been nice and friendly, there's something different about him now. He seems a little livelier, especially in his interactions with me. They've noticed the glances he and I have shared. And now they are all suggesting that this client and I should at least go out on a date.

So, Jack and I exchange numbers. We begin by talking on the phone in the evenings. Like me, he has 2 daughters and a son – in the same order as mine. And what's funny is that our kids have similarities based on their birth order. His oldest daughter is girlie, sweet, gentle, and accommodating to others. This very much defines my first-born daughter, Ashlyn. His second daughter is tomboyish yet girlie, doesn't care what others think about her, has a take it or leave it type of attitude but is still loving and considerate. This very much defines Alayna, my middle child. His son is the baby of the family, is sweet and loves his mother. Aiden isn't old enough for me to determine how he's going to be, but so far his personality seems very similar to what I've experienced with Jack's son. I can see that Jack is a phenomenal father. He cares so much for his kids. They are a priority in his life, something I have missed. His love for his children is definitely one of the things I find so attractive about him.

Like me, Jack is divorced though not for the same reasons. His wife increasingly withdrew herself from him. In fact, when Jack's dad died, instead of her accompanying him to be with him and his family, she chose to have the birthday party she had already planned for their son. At the end of that day, Jack returned home. His wife was in bed, though awake. Jack sat on the edge of the bed and just released all the emotion he had been holding in the entire day. He cried and sobbed. His heart was broken. His wife didn't so much as put her arm around him. She provided zero comfort. What kind of heartless woman would be so cold? Ultimately, their marriage just fell apart. They fell out of love, and she finally filed for divorce.

He hasn't dated much since they divorced. There have been a few women he's dated but he hasn't gone out with anyone more than 3 or 4 times. According to Jack, most of them have "daddy issues" and don't have the same goals and dreams for their lives as he does. But Jack and I seem to share similar dreams for our lives. We both love our children dearly. We both want to work to build a great life for our families. We both want to make things right and live life the honorable way. Wow! Where did this guy come from!?!

Jack and I inevitably decide to go on a date. We meet after work one Thursday night. We go to Charleston's, one of his favorites. I love the atmosphere! It is quiet and the lights are dim with a soft light over our table; very romantic. We each have a glass of wine with our dinner. We talk. We laugh. He actually listens and genuinely cares about what I have to say. And being with him is easy. It's been a long time since I've experienced something like this. To be quite honest, I don't know that it was ever this easy with Lon. This is so refreshing! And then, to top it all off, he picks up the tab!

We aren't quite ready to part ways, so we go to a quaint little bar to have another glass of wine and talk. Conversation is amazing. The chemistry is even better. As we sit there and talk, I notice that he is looking at me, almost in awe. He then tells me, "You are so pretty." At this very moment, I wonder how I got so fortunate to have met this guy. I'm on cloud nine.

We have to end our date at some point as we both have to go to work the next day. We say our goodbyes. He drives to his home and I drive to mine. I go to sleep with a smile on my face.

As the weeks go by, we continue talking on the phone every evening, we see each other at the office on Thursdays, and we go on dates Thursday nights. We try to fit in a date here and there on the weekends when I can find someone to watch the kids for a bit. Jack has made a few comments about how he'd love to be able to be a daddy to younger children again; he misses that age. His kids are in high school, junior high, and elementary. None of mine are even school age yet!

My relationship with Jack is progressing well, so we decide to get more serious. Why wouldn't we? He's amazing, thoughtful, and sensitive, and he's a great dad! Jack makes me a priority. He cares about my feelings. He's romantic. He tells me I'm pretty all the time. He's even complimentary of my French nail manicure; it is his favorite. I receive greeting cards from him in the mail at work with a $20 bill to treat myself to lunch every now and then. At least once a month, he sends me flowers. Jack has stolen my heart. I am in awe; God saved the best for last.

Seven months after we start dating, we go on a trip to Kansas City to watch a Chiefs game. Jack is a HUGE Chiefs fan. In fact, his golden retriever is named KC after the Chiefs' mascot, KC Wolf! I've never been to an NFL game before. Quite frankly, I don't really care about football, but wherever Jack is, it's where I want to be. We stay in an amazing hotel at a casino the night before the game. There are so many different restaurants and sources of entertainment. We have dinner and then, for several hours, listen to great live music. It's such a relaxing evening. The next day, we go to the Chiefs game.

I'm amazed at all the people who tailgate for hours before the game in the freezing cold weather. I'm wondering how I'm going to make it through the game in these freezing temperatures! Jack convinces me that all the people in the stands around us will help keep us warm. And actually, he was right! Shortly after halftime,

Jack calls me over to the isle of our row, as if we are going to go up the stairs and grab something to eat or drink. We hadn't talked about getting anything to eat or drink, but I'm going along with him anyway. As soon as I make it to the isle, I see 7' 2" KC Wolf. He's holding a dozen roses. I start to get light headed. KC Wolf gives me the roses and Jack gets down on one knee. He proceeds to tell me all the things he loves about me and about how he wants us to raise our children together. He asks me to marry him. Jack plans for us to become like one big Brady Bunch.

At this moment, I'm light headed *and* feeling as though I'm going to faint. I hurriedly say yes and then pull him to his feet and quickly walk back to our seats. I'm slightly embarrassed and want to get out of the spotlight as quickly as possible. However, that's impossible. After we return to our seats, everyone around us begins to congratulate us. For the remainder of the game, everyone wants to take pictures of us and pose with us. This has definitely been quite an experience! Jack never ceases to amaze me.

8 HAPPILY EVER AFTER... TEMPORARILY

Jack and I return home from our trip to Kansas City and start planning our life together. We are excited to blend our families and be the positive role models and loving parents our children deserve. We are also eager to encouragingly influence others through our marriage by putting God first, loving each other unconditionally, and staying committed to each other no matter the challenges we may face. We know blending a family is challenging, but we believe if any two people can do it, it's us!

We get plugged into a church in Tulsa, which Jack actually attended with his first wife. Yes, this sounds odd, I agree. However, because Jack speaks so highly of this church, I was open to giving it a try. And I love it! The people are amazing, and everyone is quite welcoming. They have a phenomenal kids program, and our children are excited to attend every Sunday! This in itself is priceless! The worship music is amazing. And the leadership of the church is solid; each person in leadership truly cares and is available to others. They want to do things the right way. I'm highly impressed. They have a Sunday school class for the parents of blended families, which we know will be quite beneficial for us. We've started attending this class and have already begun creating friendships with others. As we begin blending our families, we learn valuable tools to use in our own relationship. I have such peace here at this church and am thankful we have it as our church home.

Lon doesn't know much about our lives right now. He's not involved with the kids. Due to his prescription drug addition, he can only see the kids under supervision. So, he chooses not to see them at all. My precious babies don't seem to feel a void, as they now have Jack in their lives.

Three months after our engagement, it's our wedding day. We plan a small wedding and at a quaint resort outside of Tulsa inviting only a few people including my parents, my sisters, their husbands, three of his close relatives, and of course our children. I am so excited for this new chapter in my life.

However, the day doesn't start out well. My precious girls are sick – terribly sick. They both started vomiting in the wee hours of the morning and have continued throughout the day. Perhaps it's from the dinner they had last night or maybe a stomach bug. All I know is they are sick and I am not sure how to carry on with the wedding. In fact, I'm thinking this is the enemy's ploy to keep us from marrying. As a result, I am concerned we won't be able to positively affect others' lives through our marriage. I am determined to carry on and get married as planned while trying to nurse my children back to health.

We arrive at our wedding location. As soon as the girls get out of the car, they vomit on the ground. I'm torn – go home and let the enemy defeat us, interrupting our plans for our happily ever after or carry on with our ceremony quickly and get the kids home. We decide on the latter and go ahead with our wedding. Amazingly, shortly before the ceremony, the girls were better. And after the ceremony, they were able to eat dinner and seemed to feel much better. I was confident knowing I made the right choice.

Jack and I leave the next day for our honeymoon. I'm excited about a honeymoon; I didn't have one with Lon. And with 6 kids between the two of us, this is probably the only time we'll be able to get away – just the two of us – on a trip like this. We go to Coronado, an island off San Diego. It's amazingly beautiful! The ocean, the beach, the Hotel del Coronado are all stunning. What an amazing place to relax and focus on each other and our new beginning for the next 5 days and nights! I am blessed.

We chose Hotel del Coronado in which to stay because one of Jack's relatives works there and has for many years. Additionally, the hotel has such a rich history with many famous people having stayed there including various Presidents such as William Taft, Franklin Roosevelt, Ronald Reagan, Richard Nixon, Jimmy Carter, and Gerald Ford. Other famous guests have included Charlie Chapman, Charles Lindbergh, Kirk Douglas, and Marilyn Monroe.

I am pleased to meet Jack's relative, as he is an extension of my wonderful husband. I feel like meeting others in Jack's family and history help me know him more and grow closer to him. Jack's relative is not quite what I had imagined. He seems a little nervous and slightly reserved and awkward, yet he is still very nice. He generously gives us a tour of Hotel del Coronado and even takes up to the highest part of the hotel, the lighthouse, that few ever have a chance to tour, and now that special privileged few includes us. I truly feel honored.

The resort has many activities available to us, though we only spend evenings at the hotel. Our room faces the ocean, and we sleep with the door to the balcony open; I get the best sleep. All we hear is the crashing of the waves. It's so serene and so incredibly tranquil.

Over the next 5 days, we relax, walk all over Coronado Island, take naps on the beach, interact with the locals, and unwind further. We visit various restaurants and entertainment venues. We even go into San Diego to visit the Gaslamp District. It's so beautiful and clean. If we didn't have children, I could stay here forever!

Upon returning home, our life goes on as we blend two families together. I love his children dearly. They are so very sweet and respectful. And they each love my children. I'm so fortunate that blending these children has been so easy! I am certain it helps that his children are all older than mine and as a result, competition among them is nonexistent.

Over the next year, we share in various life-changing events. Jack changes positions and obtains a job at his former employer in Broken Arrow. Moving to Broken Arrow ensures we are closer to his job and our families. We decide that we are in a place financially that will allow me to stay home with the kids. So, seven months after we marry, I resign from my job to be a stay-at-home mom.

9 NOT AGAIN

I absolutely love being a stay-at-home mom. I get to cook breakfast for everyone. I am able to drop Ashlyn off at her school for kindergarten and Alayna at her school for pre-K. I am also there to pick them both up. This is a treat. During the day, I spend time with Aiden. I have the privilege and honor of taking care of our home – keeping it clean and organized – and cooking dinner every night. I develop close friendships in our neighborhood especially with my next-door neighbor, Joni, with whom I grow very close. We get up at 5 a.m. every morning to go work out, and I'm home before Jack has to leave for work. My daily schedule is fabulous – I am so thankful to spend time early in the day to take care of myself and to spend the rest of the day taking care of everyone else. Never did I think I would be a stay-at-home mom, but I definitely love it. This is what I was made to do!

An upcoming plan, another potential life-changing event, includes having Jack adopt my children. Lon is non-existent in their lives. In fact, the kids refer to Jack as "dad." Aiden doesn't even know his father. Every so often, I show a picture of his dad to him and he doesn't react whatsoever. He has no idea who the man is in the picture. In the state of Oklahoma, once a biological parent has not seen his children nor paid child support for a year, another person can adopt those children without the permission from that uninvolved biological parent. My attorney has prepared legal papers to file once we reach that one-year mark to grant Jack the ability to adopt the kids.

Other life changing events include his oldest daughter graduating from high school and getting engaged. She and I have had so much fun planning her special day. Together, we've shopped for candelabras, flowers, and even her wedding dress! I am honored to be asked to help. Some may wonder where her mom is during this time. For some reason, she has left the planning arrangements up to us, which I don't mind. It provides a bonding opportunity for the two of us. And, it allows my mom an opportunity to get involved; my mom makes all the flower arrangements for the candelabras and bouquets.

The wedding day is flawless. Everything about it is beautiful – the venue, the colors, the cake, the reception area, the dresses. I go in to see the bride before the ceremony to tell her how beautiful and special she is and to share a sentimental moment with her. As I walk in, she tells me that she *doesn't* want me in there. She makes her point come across loud and clear. I do as she wishes and leave the room. I am floored, confused, and hurt. I had a large part in planning this day with her and I am treated like this? Ok, I see how things are.

I take my seat and wait for the grandparents and mothers to be seated. I'm not escorted in to my seat as the biological moms are, and that's ok. I'm the stepmom. And at this moment, I'm feeling out of place and unwelcome. The wedding ceremony is beautiful and if I wasn't so livid, I would probably be crying because that's what I usually do at weddings. Typically, the emotion overcomes me and I cry, but not today.

The reception is nice. Everyone is sharing in conversation with one another. Each person finds their way to the bride and groom to congratulate them both. I stand to the side and stay out of the way. As the reception comes to an end and the crowd starts dwindling, I begin picking up the garbage. At this point, we have about 30 minutes to get everything cleaned up and vacate the reception hall.

As I begin taking down the decorations and centerpieces, I look around to see that no one else is helping. Not Jack. Not the ex wife. No one. This fuels my already flaming fire. I continue cleaning until it's all finished, picking up the garbage on every table. There must have been at least 20 tables!

I go outside and stand with everyone else as the bride and groom are expected to exit the building and drive off in their car decorated with the painted window exclaiming "Just Married!" As they get into the car, the bride stops and gives her dad a hug and then gets in the car. They drive away. Not once today did the bride acknowledge my presence – even as the woman who is married to her dad – much less thank me for my contribution of time, energy, and resources to this wedding. And that's ok… because it has to be.

Not once does Jack ever encourage his daughter to communicate any gratitude toward me that day or any time after. And as time goes on, I feel less and less like the step-mom and I feel more like Cinderella, the stepdaughter. The norm has recently become for Jack and his kids to make plans for the weekend and then simply inform me of what will be taking place as though I have no choice. My children and I just go along with their chosen activities. I have open conversations with Jack about my disagreement of this new norm to no avail. And although things aren't as I would like, I still love Jack and his children and will carry on.

As time goes on, I notice Jack is drinking quite a bit. When he drinks, he becomes angry. His drink of choice is vodka and Sprite. I enjoy a drink every now and then, but I don't drink excessively, nor do I change for the worse when I partake. I communicate to Jack my concerns about his drinking, and he assures me it's not a problem and that he can stop any time he wants. I've been through this addiction thing before with Lon, and although I know what he is saying is not true with addicts, I'm hopeful his words are golden. But, I'm proven wrong over and over.

On the weekend, he makes excuses to drink by taking me out "on a date" or to go dancing. Sometimes, we go watch a musician we know who performs at local venues; he is a phenomenal artist. I agree to go on these dates knowing that it is probably just an excuse for Jack to consume alcoholic beverages guilt-free. It's not like he's drinking alone when we are out, right? Well, I'm sure that's his thought process. And while his drinking is becoming an issue, I typically enjoy our nights out even though Jack drinks heavily.

However, one night is different. We go to Suede, a popular local venue, to watch the artist we know perform. We have the best seats, right in front of the dance floor. Of course, we get there early to get those seats! At one point, I have to use the restroom and on my way back to our table, I run into Jason, a guy both Jack and I know. He and I chat for a few minutes, and then I return to our seats. Jack is livid and wants to know why my trip to the restroom took so long. I explain who I ran into, yet it doesn't change Jack's demeanor. In fact, I think it worsened.

The next time I have to use the restroom, Jack thinks he needs to escort me. And escort me he does with his hand on the back of my neck forcefully guiding and directing me through the crowd. As I approach the restroom, he pushes me with his hand on the back of my neck towards the restroom door. I hear a man tell him that his conduct is inappropriate. I'm thankful for that man and his thoughts though I know that it's just going to worsen the situation. If the bathroom had a window to climb out, I might just do that at this moment. Unfortunately, I'm not so lucky. So after I'm finished, I hesitantly exit the bathroom. Of course, Jack is there waiting, visibly enraged.

Because Jack is so infuriated, he decides it's time to leave. So we leave. For some reason, we take city streets home rather than the expressway. I'm fearful of him. As we approach a red light, I quickly decide I'm going to get out of the car when we stop. I slowly reach up to the door handle to get ready to open the door. Jack must have seen that I was getting ready to get out of the car, so he speeds up and I can see he is going to run the red light. I still exit the car as planned, only the car is in motion; that wasn't part of my plan.

I roll multiple times and skid across the street getting road rash on my forearm. The contents of my purse scatter across two lanes. I grab what I can and run up to the sidewalk to avoid getting hit by an approaching car. The driver stops and the girls in the car ask if I need a ride. I should have accepted the ride, but I knew there would be hell to pay if I went with these girls. I also knew I didn't have a house key with me to get into the house. Besides, there's the issue of my children – they are home with a babysitter. Suddenly, nothing is clear. I have no idea how I'm going to get home, though I know I don't want it to be with Jack.

I walk over to Utica Square, a nearby shopping area. I go into a pharmacy that's open 24 hours and walk through the aisles trying to hide my fear and the road rash on my arm. And then I realize if Jack comes in here, he'll easily find me. So I go out and walk around the shopping area trying to find a place to hide. I see our car approaching and hear Jack saying, "Lisa, where are you?" Those words sound so frightening and eerie – just the way he said them – slow and in a super sweet though creepy tone. I kneel down and hide in bushes. Jack parks the car and begins walking around calling for me again in the same eerie tone, "Lisa, where are you?" Once again, I think about my babies at home, and I just want to be with them right now. The only way I'm going to get to them is by surrendering and riding home with Jack. I stand up revealing my hiding spot. Jack sees me and begins to approach me. He is enraged beyond any point I've ever seen. I just stand there, frozen. When he reaches me, he tries to slap my face, but only knocks the glasses off my face. I quickly pick them up, appalled he would stoop to such levels. I'm disgusted. No longer am I fearful. Well, maybe a little. Increasingly, I become livid. I finally get into the car and we go home. My shift in mood seems to halt some of his rage. The next day, nothing is said about that night, although I have never forgotten about it to this day.

Jack's alcoholism continues to affect our lives. He has started to mix his drinks in his car and then leaves the alcohol and mixed drink in his car. He hides the vodka, of course. He'll periodically go to his car to get a drink. And although vodka is known not to smell, I have news for you… It does! Not only can I smell it through his breath when he talks, but I can also smell the alcohol that seeps through his skin – the skin on his arms, his neck, and his entire body! Even our bedding smells like that sweet, alcohol smell as does our closet where he keeps his laundry hamper. It's nauseating.

Not only can I tell by the smell that Jack is drinking but also by his behavior. This evening before starting dinner, I communicate to Jack that his alcohol consumption is no secret and that his demeanor changes significantly for the worse when he drinks. He denies it as usual. While I'm cooking dinner, he gets frustrated with me because I refuse to engage in conversation with him. He's intoxicated and I just don't want to hear anything that comes out of his mouth – more excuses and empty promises. Because I am not participating in the conversation, Jack grabs the pot of spaghetti that is cooking and throws it out the back door, and then proceeds to yell at me. Yes, he just discarded the dinner I've been making for my kids. And he's not helping his case with his rage and fury. At this point, I simply continue to ignore him and begin making another meal for my children.

Once again, nothing is said about that night, but of course, I have never forgotten about it. This incident reminds me all too well of that night near Utica Square.

We still attend our home church, and we still attend the Blended Families Sunday School class. The problem is Jack isn't transparent with the challenges he faces including alcoholism. How can others provide him with support and accountability if he isn't honest with others, much less himself?

I fought for my marriage with Lon, and we all know how that ended. And here I am with Jack – an alcoholic who won't admit his problem and as a result, our marriage is failing. How did I get here? I refuse to have another failed marriage and won't give up. I'll continue to fight. I'll continue to love him. After all, love is a verb, not always a feeling. Besides, there are great things about him. Some of the great things I love about him include the way he loves our kids – his and mine. He loves to have fun with them and hear them laugh. He plays with them. He showers them with attention. When things are good, they are great.

Another thing I love about Jack is his discontentment with injustice towards children. The news about the disappearance of Jessica Lunsford in Florida has us glued to the television. And as the news announces that a registered sex offender is responsible for the kidnapping and murder of Jessica, both Jack and I feel disgusted. In fact, Jack is enraged. We both feel such helplessness for these types of victims. This is so unfair – a monster hurting powerless, innocent children. We are both in mourning for Jessica and for her family. Neither of us could even begin to imagine such a tragedy happening to our own children. When something like this happens, you hold your children a little closer and hug them a little tighter.

I know there are sexual predators and offenders in the world. And because of this, I have always talked to my children about such people. Since Ashlyn was a tiny baby, during bath time, even before she could understand me, I would tell her while identifying areas about which I was talking, "These are your personal areas. Other people are not allowed to touch you in these areas. If anyone touches you in these areas, you say, 'Stop! I'm telling my mom!' And then I want you to come tell me! No one can touch you – not your dad, not Papa, not Nana, not Grandpa, not Grandma." I would go through an entire list of everyone. I even said, "And if I touch you in your personal areas, you need to tell your dad, or Papa, or Nana, or Grandpa, or Grandma."

And as she got older, I would have her role-play, telling me, "Stop! I'm going to tell my mommy!" I wanted to get her comfortable with saying those words so that she could say them if she was ever in such a situation. We discussed the topic during every bath experience. And as Alayna and Aiden were born, I shared the same dialogue and role playing with them. I began adding questions every now and then, and not necessarily during bath time, asking, "Has anyone touched you in your personal area?" To my relief, they always answered in their precious, little, high-pitched voices, "No, mommy." I thought I had covered it all. But I hadn't.

10 THE DISCOVERY

As previously mentioned, Jack and I have discussed the likelihood of him adopting my children. Of course, I feel great about this when alcohol isn't a factor. But recently, the drinking has gotten worse, however I'm hopeful that as we continue to attend church and our Blended Families Sunday School class, he will make the decision to quit drinking. I'm not oblivious, but I am hopeful. Next week will mark a year since Lon has had contact with us. And next week, the attorney plans to file those adoption papers. I would like to see positive changes immediately with Jack, as this would make me feel better about going forward with the adoption process.

*****

Lo and behold, Lon calls over the weekend asking if he can see the kids. During the phone call, Lon acknowledges his absence for the past year. He also states that he is at our mercy and will abide by whatever standards and boundaries we set forth in order for him to see his children. And if seeing the children in our home under our supervision is the only way in which he is able to see the children, then he will happily oblige.

Of course, I'm shocked. His timing could not be any worse! Just one more week, and he would no longer have parental rights. Jack is upset and disapproving. He goes as far as to say, "I'm their dad now." While I understand Jack's feelings, I also understand that no one can ever truly take the place of their biological dad. Their little hearts would always have a void and they would always be curious about their dad. At some point, they would choose to know him. That didn't make Jack feel better. As a result of Lon's re-emergence, a wedge is beginning to make its way into my marriage, even more so than before. In truth, it wasn't so much Lon's presence as it was the inability for Jack and me to agree on the appropriate way to move forward.

Because our marriage is strained, Jack and I seek marriage counseling through our church. We are referred to a marriage counselor and attend together for three visits. Each time, Jack downplays his drinking – the amount and frequency of his alcohol consumption. I'm hopeful the counselor sees through his lies. We also discuss Lon's renewed desire to be a part of his children's lives. The counselor sees no harm in this and ultimately believes developing a relationship with him is what's best for the kids. Jack disagrees. A few weeks after we start counseling, Jack decides he no longer wants to attend. And while he no longer wants to attend, I keep praying for God to do something miraculous for Jack and for our marriage.

*****

The children have changed so much over the past year. Ashlyn is now 6. She's just so precious. Her smile is huge and her heart is even bigger! She is so accommodating to others including her brother and sister. Whatever they want, she gives it to them. If she is playing with a toy they want, she happily hands it over. I have tried to communicate to her that she doesn't have to give up her toys to her younger siblings and she can play with the toys she chooses, but she never does. One day, I'm hopeful she will learn that it's ok not to be so accommodating to others and to allow herself the opportunity to do what *she* wants.

Alayna is 4, almost 5. She is so talkative that it seems she is only silent when asleep! Her curly hair is adorable as are her deep dimples. She tells everyone her name is Peter Parker, as she truly believes she is Spiderman! In fact, in order for her to respond, I have to call her "Peter Parker." And if I don't, she is sure to correct me by saying, "I'm not Alayna! I'm Peter Parker!"

Aiden is 2, almost 3. He loves to dance! We all dance every day after school. And, Aiden and I dance every evening while I'm cooking dinner. I sweep him up in my arms and we dance and dance and dance. He loves it! I love it! His disposition is so gentle and kind. Yet, he can hold his own with his sisters. They definitely love and protect him.

I'm so blessed to have these precious babies in my life. Lon sure has missed out. And for that, I am sorry. I am sorry for his loss. There is nothing more precious than these children, who they are, who they become every day. It is an incredible experience watching them develop and learn, while discovering the world.

*****

Ashlyn and I are in the car running errands. She is in her booster seat in the middle of the back seat. She loves sitting in the middle so that she can see everything not just through the side windows but also directly ahead of us. She's always been very observant, taking everything in. I love looking at her in the rearview mirror. I love watching her as she observes and explores the world around her. I also love being able to look at her when she and I are talking. Being able to see her captivating expressions is priceless.

As I often do, I take advantage of the one on one time to talk about a variety of subjects. I mention her dad since he seems to be coming back into the picture. She is excited at the thought of seeing him, although I sense some nervousness. I decide to let that subject subside for now and move on to something else. I then ask her a question that is typically a part of our dialogue: "Has anyone touched you in your personal areas?" She was quick to answer no, but there was an uneasiness in her answer. Her demeanor was different this time than any other time when she has previously answered this question. Perhaps it was because we just talked about her dad and she was still working through those emotions. But

Ashlyn did not confidently tell me "no," that someone had not touched her.

I had to explore this subject, either way. Immediately, another question came to mind that I had never previously considered. "Has anyone made you touch them in their personal areas?" I just have to ask it. So I do. And I am not ready for the response. No mother is ever ready to hear this response. With reluctance, Ashlyn says, "Yes." My heart starts racing. A million thoughts are simultaneously going through my mind. I'm trying to remain calm and inviting to her answers, but inside I'm a complete mess. And then I ask who did this to her. She responds, "Daddy." Which daddy? Jack? Lon? How did this happen? When did this happen? To what extent? How could I have not known? I ask her, "Daddy Jack or Daddy Lon?"

"Daddy Jack."

The breath is literally knocked out of me. Every muscle in my body is limp. In a matter of one second, my world has just been turned upside down. Moreover, I realize my precious Ashlyn's world has been turned upside down.

I communicate to Ashlyn that I will look into this. I cannot conceive how this could ever happen. I am at a loss for direction. But I need help and only know one person I can trust who is non-biased. She is a counselor who attends our church. Actually, she is not yet technically a counselor, but is working towards becoming a counselor. She is under supervision to obtain her license to practice. However I trust her and I know she will provide me with sound, professional guidance.

Once I'm alone, I contact her and share the details of my conversation with Ashlyn. The counselor and I discuss all the changes that are taking place including Lon coming back into our lives. We talk about how I "led" Ashlyn by asking questions rather than allowing her to tell me on her own terms. The counselor advises that Ashlyn's answer could be attention-seeking behavior. She shares that she herself was molested and in her opinion, Ashlyn doesn't exhibit the same typical signs as victims of child molestation. The counselor knows Jack and our family and believes that Jack could never do this to a child. So I ask for her professional advice on how to move forward. She suggests that Jack, Ashlyn, and I all sit down to talk about the consequences of lying about such a serious offense. I take the counselor's advice.

I sit Jack down to inform him of the accusations and the advice I received from the counselor on how to handle the situation. Jack is initially upset that I didn't go to him first, but is thankful for the direction provided by such a professional. We decide to have this discussion with Ashlyn in our bedroom. We call Ashlyn in and have her sit with us on our bed. I explain that I spoke with a woman we know and trust about the statements she made about Jack having her touch him inappropriately. Jack proceeds to tell Ashlyn how telling such a lie can break up our family. During this conversation, Ashlyn is visibly uncomfortable. She does not want to make eye contact with either of us. I thought about how I would feel having such a conversation with my parents, and I would not want to look at them either.

A few weeks go by. Jack's behavior has become so erratic and his words so piercing that I feel like I am on a roller coaster. Jack's drinking has worsened both in frequency and amount. I have become fearful of him, more so than ever before. He increasingly becomes less and less tolerable. He resents my initiation of any conversations concerning the potential of Lon seeing the kids. He is absolutely refusing to let Lon visit them. Jack even goes so far as to accuse me of wanting Lon back, which he states is the reason he believes I'm pushing for Lon and the kids to be reunited.

Getting back with Lon is the farthest from my mind. It's all about my children seeing their father and developing a relationship with him. Yes, he has been a drug addict. And yes, he has been absent and not a part of their lives. But he should not be punished, per se, because of his past mistakes. He has a right to see his children and they have a right to know him.

A couple more weeks go by. It's a Tuesday morning, July 26th. Jack is outraged, this time with no discernible trigger. We had not discussed Lon or the children. Yet, Jack proceeds to yell at me about his perception of my desire to sleep with Lon. He then calls me inexcusable names and questions my loyalty, commitment, and fidelity to him and our marriage. He begins throwing things in the closet and in the bathroom. The entire time, he has a brooding look in his eyes. It's a very dark and scary look. The moment he leaves for work, I call my mom and tell her, "I'm moving out today. I don't know where I'm going, but I'm moving out. Even if I have to go to a homeless shelter, I will. We can't stay here."

Of course, my mom is blindsided, as she has no idea there are problems in my marriage. Remember, I became a pro at hiding my marital problems when Lon and I were together. I share with my mom the details of Jack's alcoholism and how fearful I had become. She immediately calls my dad and some family friends. Within an hour, my dad and their friends are at my house with trucks and trailers to move me out. Meanwhile, my mom is looking for a house for me to rent close to her and my dad in a suburb north of Tulsa.

She found a small rent house for us just a few miles from their home. It's vacant and available immediately. God's provision is amazing! We get all of our stuff packed and all of our furniture loaded within 2 1/2 hours. Our stuff is moved in and unpacked before Jack even gets home from work. Though I knew the minute he got home to our empty house, as he began calling my phone repeatedly. It feels as though I am prey being stalked. I refuse to answer.

Jack continues to call, leaving messages, stating that he misses me and will do whatever he needs to make our marriage work. He also says he will stop drinking. However, in the very next message, he says I'm a whore and accuses me of leaving him for Lon. Every message is different. I don't want to hear his empty promises or false accusations, and I don't want to go on the rollercoaster rides he's obviously on. So I stop listening to his messages and simply delete them as soon as he leaves them.

It's been about 2 weeks since the kids and I escaped to a small little home in the town in which my parents live. I hate this place. I hate this town. This house will never feel like home to me. This town will never feel like home to me. I'm in such a transitional period in my life, and never have I felt so directionless or so alone. I have been searching for jobs, but am still unemployed. I have no idea where I'm going to get the money to pay rent, how I'm going to pay for groceries, or even buy school clothes for my children. This moment is difficult for me because I am a person with direction and I always have been. I'm independent. I take care of business. That's who I am. Being without direction and not knowing anything about tomorrow is foreign to me. It's grueling.

Because I want my babies to relax and just be children, not think about Jack or their dad or how our lives are falling apart, I often take them outside to play. In fact, we play outside every day. But today is different. Ashlyn, my sweet precious 6 year old, is full of anger. As she rides her bike around the driveway, she stops, tightens her fists, clenches her jaw and says, "I'm so glad Jack is not my stepdad!" The degree of her rage is concerning. I wonder if her rage has anything to do with the allegations she made previously about Jack. I decide immediately to get her into counseling, as I'm not a professional and have no idea how to even begin to handle this. Thank God for counselors who can help children!

We are introduced a phenomenal counselor through Family and Children's Services (FCS) who is sweet, kind, and gentle and whom Ashlyn immediately trusts. I truly believe if anything needs to be revealed, it will be revealed with this counselor.

*****

Four weeks after leaving Jack, I started a job! I went back to my roots and went back into recruiting. I am thankful that someone gave me an opportunity after being a stay-at-home-mom for a year! After all, I have 3 kids and a household for which to provide! Two days after starting my job, I started school to finish my Bachelor's. I am determined to never let not having a Bachelor's degree ever keep me from obtaining a job again! It has never taken me that long, that many applications, that many resume submissions, and that many interviews to get a job.

The kids have also started school. I'm thankful that our move was made at the end of the summer so that my kids were able to start school at the beginning of the school year. Ashlyn is in 1st grade and Alayna is in kindergarten. Aiden is only 3 and is cared for by a wonderful woman in her home.

Jack files for divorce. And, he wants his furniture back. He and I still have not talked on the phone but have corresponded via email making arrangements for me to sign divorce papers and get his furniture back to him without me having to see him. He rents a U-Haul and meets my brother-in-law with it along with our divorce papers for me to sign. My brother-in-law brings the U-Haul to my home, and he and my dad load the furniture. I review and sign the divorce papers. And then my brother-in-law delivers the papers and truck back to Jack.

Later in the evening, the kids go to bed and I sit in my living room in a borrowed lawn chair looking around at all that I don't have. I don't have a TV, a couch, living room furniture, or a kitchen table. I don't even have a bed, a mattress, or a dresser. I continue to think about other things I don't have like the stress of Jack's controlling behavior or having to deal with his alcoholism. I don't have to be nervous in my own home anymore wondering what kind of mood Jack will be in when he wakes up or when he gets home.

I think about what I do have – peace, my precious babies, a roof over my head, a job, a car that gets me to work, food in my pantry, money to pay my bills, my health, and my faith. I have so much for which to be thankful. And I will sit here with an attitude of thanksgiving because I am truly thankful.

*****

All is going well. I love my job and the people with whom I work! I've received a few paychecks, which have helped me get on my feet. I love my babies and am able to fully enjoy them without any stressors in the home.

Ashlyn seems to be doing better. She's been in counseling for about a month. I'm thankful my younger sister is available and willing to get her to and from her counseling appointments, as I really am not in a position to be missing work.

I receive a call at work late in the afternoon from Ashlyn's counselor. Ashlyn told her story… Her story about being violated by Jack. Once again, the breath was knocked out of me. But this time I had direction. Ashlyn's counselor provided me with that direction… appropriate direction. She advised me to file a police report, as this was a criminal act. Not once had I ever comprehended this as a criminal act. Not once had I considered going to the police. Not once had I considered turning him in. Previously, I had been in panic mode without clear thoughts and clear understanding of how to handle such a situation. However, this is the case no longer. I now know what I must do.

And thus began the fight of our lives.

11 THE FIGHT OF OUR LIVES

I finally have saved enough money to buy a few things for our home. My sister's friends own storage units and when tenants don't pay their rental fees, my sister's friends sell the contents in the storage units. I am able to buy a bedroom suite, a washing machine, and a kitchen table. Lon's parents gave me a couch, love seat, and two tables for the living room. Things are coming together for us. My house is finally feeling like a home. But, I still hate this town. I feel like a foreigner here. Nothing about this town feels like home. I don't have to be here forever, but it does work for us for now.

Although I know God's hand is all over my life and He has provided for us, I can't bring myself to pray. I don't have the energy to pray. I can't open my Bible. I can't even listen to Christian music. I don't understand why. I just know that I can't.

This situation has sucked all the strength from me. Putting on a façade of being strong for the kids and the rest of my family since the move has sucked the energy out of me. I'm so prideful and private that even my family doesn't know how broken I am because of all that has transpired. I'm exhausted. Sometimes, I don't even have the energy to make dinner, and the kids eat cereal or sandwiches for dinner. Sometimes, the dishes pile in the sink for two days because I don't have the energy to clean them. All of my energy is used for the basics right now; getting out of bed, taking a shower, getting the kids ready for school, going to work, picking the kids up after work, and taking them home. We spend our evenings talking and laughing. Then they take their baths. After they get in bed, I tuck them in. I kiss their eyes so that they will have sweet dreams. And then I tell them I love them "so muchie, muchie, muchie." After the nighttime routine, I collapse on the coach. I take several slow, deep breaths. And then I get up and start reviewing my bank account just to ensure there is no fraudulent activity as I'm now paranoid about identify theft. After checking, I move on to my homework.

As advised by Ashlyn's counselor, I am taking her to file a police report in the city in which we lived when the incident occurred. On the way there, I am praying that God will give her courage through this process. Upon arrival, we meet with two male police officers, as they do not have a female police officer available. They give her a stuffed rabbit, dressed in a police officer uniform complete with a badge. They also give Ashlyn her very own police badge.

The police officers are incredible. They are supportive of us yet disgusted about our situation. They speak in code (so that Ashlyn won't understand) about what they want to do to Jack. They furnish me with the forms to provide a written statement. It takes me about 30 minutes to complete the process. They wish us luck and we leave.

Within a few days, a detective assigned to our case contacts me. She is serious and direct, yet empathetic. She is disturbed that a man would do such a horrendous thing to such a young child. I hesitate to even call him a man. Right now, I consider him a monster. He's a wolf in sheep's clothing. The detective explains that she wants to speak to Jack, but won't contact him until I get a protective order. She directs me to immediately obtain a protective order and to let her know once it is obtained. She also advised me that I couldn't talk to Ashlyn about Jack. I cannot ask her questions about what happened to her. And if she tries to talk to me about it, I have to stop her and inform her that she has to share those things with her counselor. If Ashlyn and I discuss any part of her experience, we could hinder the prosecution's case.

The process of getting a protective order is uncomfortable. I have to explain Ashlyn's story to the advocate at Domestic Violence Intervention Services (DVIS) assisting me with the paperwork. I then have to explain the situation to a judge in front of other individuals in the room also requesting a protective order. The judge is kind. I can see the concern she has for Ashlyn and me without her even saying a word. She doesn't ask a lot of questions and quickly grants an emergency protective order. With this protective order, he is ordered not to contact me or Ashlyn in any way and must remain 300 yards away from us at all times. I am to return in two weeks for a permanent protective order.

The next step in the process is for Jack to be served with the protective order. Not only will he receive the protective order, but he will also receive all of the details I provided. Soon, he will know that I know what he did to Ashlyn. He will know I filed a police report. He will know that Ashlyn is seeing a counselor. He will also know a detective has been assigned to this case. Before the detective can even contact him for questioning, he will have all of this information. The report is in my handwriting. I'm disgusted at the thought of him even seeing my handwriting. I don't understand why; I just am.

I contact the detective and inform her that I have obtained an emergency protective order. I ask her to follow up with me about the details of her conversation with Jack. In the meantime, I take copies of the protective order to Ashlyn's school per the advice of the advocate at DVIS. I inform them of our current circumstances. I also take a copy of the protective order to Ashlyn's childcare provider and give her an explanation as well.

After leaving the childcare provider, the kids and I go home. We go through our normal evening routine of dinner and baths, and I make sure they are tucked into bed. I then sit down to review my bank account. As I previously explained, I review the bank account daily to review the transitions of the day and ensure there is no fraudulent activity. However, this night is different. While reviewing my bank account, I realize I have not yet made my car payment for this month. As soon as I moved about two months ago, I contacted the finance company and provided a change of address. I have since received a statement and made a payment. Yet, I haven't received any other statements. With all the stress in my life, I was counting on the statement to remind me to make the payment.

The next day, I contact the finance company to communicate the reason I had not yet made a payment and to determine why I hadn't received another statement. The customer service rep explains to me that my "husband" called in to change my address and stated that the address on file was wrong. I ask the customer service rep for the specific date he called. She tells me it's been within the past month. I'm devastated, disheartened, discouraged, disgusted, and scared because I realize that he now knows my address. In the state of Oklahoma with regards to any debt, employees in call centers cannot give any personal information to anyone, even a spouse – unless that person is on the loan. I know this because my mom worked in collections for multiple years. The customer service rep who is helping me feels terrible about the situation and explains that perhaps it happened because the call center is located in a different state. At this point, it doesn't matter. What matters is Jack now knows where I live. I no longer have even a remote sense of safety.

It's after 11 PM and the kids are asleep. I'm asleep. The doorbell rings. I immediately wake up in a panic. I don't want to look outside. I'm afraid to see who it might be. I sit up, but am frozen. I can't move. My heart is racing. My breathing is heavy. I am sweating. I wonder if it is Jack out there. And if it is, I wonder if I call the police, will they get here before he breaks in and hurts us?

The doorbell rings again. Quietly and slowly, I get up and look out the window. Gradually, I comprehend that there is a sheriff's car in front of my house. I quickly run to the front door to find two sheriffs standing there. They inform me they are there to serve a protective order to Jack. I introduce myself as the one who filed the protective order and that they need to serve him at his residence, not mine. The courthouse gave these sheriffs the wrong address to serve the protective order! The kind sheriffs apologize for waking me and reassure me that Jack will be served.

I can't go back to sleep because I know that he hasn't yet been served. I also realize that he knows where I live. I grasp the fact that, since he hasn't been served, there is nothing preventing him from contacting me via phone, email, or even in person.

A few days later, the detective contacts me. She informs me that Jack has finally been served with the protective order and that she tried to contact him. However, he has refused to talk to her. Jack advised the detective that she could contact his attorney directly. So that's that. He's already contacted his attorney. He's already planning his defense.

Two weeks after my request for an emergency protective order, I return for the permanent protective order hearing. Of course, Jack doesn't show. I'm relieved I don't have to see him. I believe this should therefore be an easy process and my request for a permanent protective order should be granted. Wrong! Because there is an ongoing criminal investigation, the courts won't grant a permanent protective order. I discover that for the duration of this criminal investigation, I have to return to court every three weeks for the continuance of the protective order. Unbelievable! I will have to miss half a day of work every three weeks for this. Remember, I'm new at my job. Being in HR, I know how important it is to have excellent attendance. I'd be shocked if my employer doesn't terminate me over the absences that have already occurred and now the absences expected in the future! I'll be so very grateful if they decide to keep me, but shocked!

The detective contacts me and explains I need to take Ashlyn to Child Abuse Network (CAN) for a forensic interview. She explains the process and provides me with an understanding of what I should expect. Ashlyn will be taken into a room with a counselor whom she has never met and she will answer questions about the case. Meanwhile, the detective will be on the other side of a two-way mirror observing the interaction. The counselor will provide her professional opinion as to whether or not she believes that Ashlyn has been the victim of sexual abuse. The meeting and findings will be documented and sent to the detective.

Everyone at CAN is wonderful. They are welcoming with soft, warm smiles. The lobby is colorful and bright. Toys and books for kids of every age are found throughout the waiting area. I speak briefly with Ashlyn and explain she will be meeting with a very nice lady. I explain to Ashlyn that she needs to answer the questions truthfully. I also tell her I'll be sitting in the waiting room and will see her as soon as she is finished with her meeting.

For the 45 minutes that Ashlyn is with the counselor, I sit and think about how we got here. I cannot believe I allowed someone do this to her. I made a decision that allowed someone into our family who violated her. This man was invited into our family, into the lives of my children by me. The person who ultimately stole the innocence from my daughter was someone I allowed into our lives. How could she ever forgive me? What kind of mother am I? I'm the one who is supposed to protect my children more than anyone else in their lives. And yet, somehow, I failed to protect Ashlyn. *I failed to protect her. I failed her.*

Then, I think about the conversation she and I had a few months ago when I led her in a series of questions. I think about the bad advice I got from my counselor friend on how to handle the situation. I think about the conversation and how I made Ashlyn endure the conversation with Jack and me. I am mortified by how frightening that must have been for her. Then I think about Lon and how we wouldn't be sitting here if he would never have become addicted to drugs. I'm so angry. I'm angry with Lon for his choices. I'm angry with myself. I'm infuriated with Jack. And I haven't had one moment to truly process any of this.

Ashlyn comes out of her forensic interview. The detective

advises she will call me with more information.

Ashlyn and I then go to Sonic for a treat. She deserves so much more than Sonic. She deserves the world. This strong, courageous little girl deserves the world. But for now, Sonic will have to do. While we are sitting at Sonic, Ashlyn is in the back seat in middle and I can see her perfectly in the rear view mirror. I turn on the radio. A song immediately comes on that encourages listeners to come out of hiding from whatever circumstances they are in and to be empowered to stand strong in their situation and move forward. I look at Ashlyn and say, "Ashlyn, you can do this. I'm right here with you." It's a milestone moment.

It's been a long day. I don't have the energy for my schoolwork, so I choose to go to bed. I feel so alone. No one really, truly knows I am so hurt and alone. Nor do I tell anyone how hurt and alone I am. It feels like I don't even know who I am anymore. I'm no longer strong. I feel so incredibly weak that I am lying on my side in the fetal position like a baby. While I know that God will not leave me nor forsake me, I pray for Him to just wrap His arms around me and comfort me. I ask Him to hold me. I ask Him to help me. And He does. Immediately, I feel comfort and warmth. It's as though I can feel Him wrap His arms all around me and hold me close. I begin to cry. I am crying about the hurts, the violations, the betrayals, and the challenges of having to be strong when I am really very weak. I'm crying about my life. Two failed marriages. One ex-husband is a drug addict while the other is a child molester who violated my daughter. I'm only 28, and this is my life. This is my life!

I'm a single mom of three precious babies deserving of so much more than I can give and have given them. I pray that God protects their hearts and their minds. I want to pray for so much more, but that's all that I have the strength to pray for at this moment. Although I haven't talked to God for the past few months, I thank Him that He's been there. I know He's been there waiting for me to call on Him. And now, He's here with me.

*****

On December 5th, the charges of sexual assault against Jack are finally filed in Tulsa County. His bond is set at $100,000. He turns himself in but doesn't spend a moment in jail, as his aunt, a doctor with plenty of money, provides him the money needed for bail. Jack's arraignment is scheduled for January 30th.

While preparing for the arraignment, the detective discovers Jack had another victim six years ago. That victim was 12 years old at the time. She was his daughter's friend and one of their neighbors. She was staying the night with Jack's daughter. After everyone was asleep, Jack went upstairs and approached his daughter's sleeping friend. He placed her hand on his genitals. His daughter's friend woke up during this and demanded to go home. She did indeed go home in the middle of the night. This very occurrence is most likely the real reason for his divorce. I'm appalled that his ex-wife never told me about the situation. She should have told me mother-to-mother so that I could have protected my daughter. How dare she conceal such information! Absolutely inexcusable! Yet, while absolutely inexcusable, I still do not blame her for what happened.

Jack's previous victim is now 18. Her parents didn't and wouldn't make her testify against him. So he practically got away with it. The victim and her parents moved out of state shortly thereafter to get away from Jack. The victim told the detective she would be willing to come back and testify against Jack during the trial. Her testimony strengthens our case. I'm so incredibly thankful the victim is willing to testify.

During the arraignment, Jack pleads not guilty. We are set to return on February 23rd for the preliminary hearing. Ashlyn now has to prepare for her potential upcoming court appearance.

To prepare for court, Ashlyn meets with the District Attorney, Neil, and an advocate from CASA, Court Appointed Special Advocates. Ashlyn has to tell them her story. I'm so very thankful for her advocate from CASA, as she helps Ashlyn feel as comfortable as she can through this process, especially considering that this is the first time Ashlyn has to tell her story to a man. She has to answer questions they ask - the same type of questions she'll be asked in the courtroom. From this moment forward, the DA, her advocate, her counselor, and our detective refer to her experience as "Ashlyn's story" which provides her some sort of empowerment.

Ashlyn also attends court school provided by CAN (Child Abuse Network) for children who are victims in criminal cases. During court school, she learns where the judge sits in the courtroom. She also learns where Jack will sit and where she will sit when she testifies. I'm told that I cannot be in the courtroom when she testifies. I'm mortified and once again disgusted. My precious Ashlyn who is only 7 years old will not only have to testify in a room full of strangers, but she will also have to identify Jack by pointing to him when asked. She has to face this alone. Without me! This is infuriating! Jack seems to have more rights than my daughter whom he chose to violate, chose to rob of her childhood, and chose to force to grow up faster than she should have. Our system fails these helpless, precious, innocent children.

While we have a system that fails our children, there is a phenomenal group, BACA (Bikers Against Child Abuse), a non-profit that helps children who are victims of abuse feel safe and supported. BACA learns of Ashlyn's story and chooses to adopt her as a little BACA sister. The adoption experience is exciting and overwhelming! Over 100 bikers greet Ashlyn at our home. The rumbling of the motorcycles could be heard for miles and about 5 minutes before their arrival. In fact, when BACA is scheduled to have an adoption of a child, they contact the local police department to make them aware of their upcoming visit.

During the visit, the bikers each greet all three children. Ashlyn is introduced to her appointed big BACA brother and sister. It's been an experience, as none of my children have been around bikers. On the surface, bikers can seem intimidating. However, my children quickly warm up to these amazing bikers, as they are all so gentle, friendly, warm, and kind. They volunteer their time and resources to help children. They volunteer their time to ensure these children feel safe and supported so that these children can be empowered to continue through the court process.

The BACA bikers reassure Ashlyn that they will be at the courthouse for each court hearing. Her BACA brothers and sisters explain that everywhere she turns, she will see them wearing their BACA patches. When she sees them in their BACA patches, she will know they won't let anyone hurt her there. They also reassure Ashlyn that they will be present in the courtroom. They tell her she will see them in their BACA vests when she enters the courtroom and can be assured they will protect her there as well. This helps Ashlyn feel empowered and helps energize her to go the distance.

On February 23rd, we arrive for the preliminary hearing only to be told that Jack's attorney requested more time. We have to return on March 23rd.

On March 23rd, we return to court. Once again, Jack's attorney requests a pass. We have to return on April 20th.

On April 20th, we return. Jack's attorney has requested another pass. We are advised to return on May 1st.

On May 1st, we return. It's no surprise to hear that Jack's attorney has asked for another pass. We are advised to return on May 8th.

On May 8th, we return. Jack's attorney requests another pass. We are told to return on June 12th.

On June 12th, we return. Jack's attorney requests yet another pass. We are told to return on July 18th.

On July 13th, I receive a call informing me that our court hearing has been passed to August 8th.

On August 8th, Jack pleads not guilty once again. Ashlyn does not have to testify. We are advised to return for a jury trial on March 1st. March 1st! That's over 6 months from now! That's six more months our lives are on hold. That's six more months that we are forced to wait. It will be six more months before we can truly leave this behind us and move forward with our lives.

One month before the trial, Ashlyn tells me she doesn't want to testify. She's tired and she wants to move beyond this. She wants to forget it. She doesn't want to have to deal with it or think about it anymore. Yet, due to the delays, she has been forced to think about it and deal with it over the past year's court hearings. Also, she had to attend court school and her continued weekly counseling appointments. I call Ace, Ashlyn's big BACA brother, for help. I tell him Ashlyn doesn't want to testify. He asks to speak with her. Ashlyn talks to Ace for about five minutes. As she gives the phone back to me, she says, "I'm ready. I'll do it." Ace explains to me that he told Ashlyn, "You have to do this. You have to do this for you. You have to do this so that he can't hurt anyone else again." I tell Ace how thankful I am for him. He gave Ashlyn the encouragement she needs to face this next month of preparation for trail. God puts different people in our lives for different reasons. Ace was put in our lives to give Ashlyn the courage and the strength to continue with this ridiculously drawn-out case.

Because it's been over a year since Ashlyn went through court school, I reenroll her to attend again. She needs to be ready to testify.

After attending court school for the second time, she is quite confident. She even demonstrates how she will point him out in the courtroom. She adds a little attitude in her demonstration. I'm so very proud of her. What an incredible, precious soul.

The week of February 7th, I receive a call from Neil, the District Attorney. He regretfully explains that a law was just passed that won't allow Jack's former victim to testify in court. The timeframe of her experience exceeds the timeframe deemed acceptable in the new law. As a result, we've just lost the opportunity to present testimony from our key witness. We've just lost what would have made the most significant difference in this case. Regardless, we must move on as determined as ever, and perhaps even more so now.

It's the week of February 14th. I receive another call from Neil. This time he asks me what I want out of this case. I think about it for a moment, then explain to Neil that if I could only have one thing, it would be for Jack to have to register as a sex offender. I would love for him to serve time in prison, but I'll settle for him registering as a sex offender. And ultimately, I would prefer if Ashlyn didn't have to testify. Preventing or reducing the potential trauma of her having to testify would be a Godsend. She's been through so much. This has been ridiculously drawn out. She's ready for this to be put behind us. If I can spare her from having to see him and testify against him and still obtain a favorable conviction and ultimately justice for Ashlyn, it would be an incredible blessing. Neil ends the call by promising to call me back once he has more direction.

On February 22nd, I receive another call from Neil. He very gently says, "Lisa, it's over." I replay that sentence in my head a few times before it actually registers. And then I realize, it really is over. I am in total disbelief. I cannot believe this day has come. Neil continues, "Jack took a plea agreement. He has pled guilty. He'll be on a suspended sentence, but he'll have to check in with a probation officer. And he'll have to register as a sex offender." I reply with exhausted excitement. While this might sound contradictory, it is such a perfect description. I reply, "Neil, thank you for all you've done for Ashlyn!" Neil's perseverance, guidance, and expertise have helped us navigate through this nightmare. I will, for the rest of my life, be grateful to and thankful for Neil.

We end our conversation and I hang up the phone. I get up and close my office door. Sitting at my desk, I begin to cry. I finally get to release all the emotions I couldn't quite let go over the past year and a half. And let me just say, there is a lot to release! I cannot believe it's finally over. For 30 solid minutes, I continue crying. I'm so thankful that God got us through this nightmare. I'm so thankful we have a conviction. I'm so thankful Ashlyn didn't have to testify. I'm thankful we can finally move on with our lives. I'm so thankful for my precious children. I'm just so very thankful.

12 LIFE AFTER CHAOS

After finally receiving a conviction, we were finished dealing with the issue. Although Ashlyn and I could now actually talk about the events and details of what happened to her, we didn't want to. We wanted to leave it in the past, though we did have the understanding that she could talk about it at any time.

For a year and a half while dealing with the court case, we were not able to move forward in our lives. Everything was at a standstill. Most days, Ashlyn had to try to forget what happened to her, but when speaking to the prosecuting attorney or when preparing for court, she would have to recall all of the details. Now, she no longer has to. I had been under such tremendous emotional stress, and that stress persisted all the way through the day of the relieving conviction. Without such stress, I had to learn to live again. It was good. It felt foreign to be stress free, but it was good.

Lon is seeing the kids regularly – every other weekend and every Wednesday night. The kids need that. And really, I need that. I'm still attending school, and of course working full-time. I have started enjoying the company of my friends on the weekends – not every weekend but at least once a month. We go to the movies, various local events, live music venues, and of course, out to eat. Looking back, I realized I had lost myself during the trial. My life was on hold. I had no idea who I was as a person or what I wanted in life. I had been strictly in survival mode, living one day at a time with no planning ahead. How could anyone plan ahead while being stuck daily reliving a nightmare until finally there was an end with closure? My goal was to make it through to the end of the court case, and I had reached my goal. Now what?

Although at this point, I am anti-male, anti-dating and anti-marriage for obvious reasons, I have gone on a few dates that have been set up by loved ones. It is mortifying. I feel in my heart that I will not share my life with another man, and I am perfectly fine with that. These dating experiences, however, have proven to be entertaining stories to share with others, even though they are humiliating for me. Of course, when I go on these dates, I meet the guy at the location of our date. No way is one of these guys coming to my home. No one is going to know where I live. I will not get in a vehicle with anyone. I'll enjoy someone's company, maybe, and then safely leave on my own.

Some of these dates have been complete wrecks. Let's see. There was one blind date set up by someone very close to me. We met at Chili's in Owasso. This guy put so much hairspray on his super short 80's style hair that it made his forehead and scalp shiny. I was almost blinded by the shine. He was somewhat goofy. Nothing about him screamed, "Great guy for Lisa." Nothing. He reminded me of the character Harry Dunne in the movie "Dumb and Dumber." Even his disposition and personality were similar to Harry's. In fact, if he was an actor, he would definitely be spot on for Harry. For those who know me, they know this is so not the right fit for me. I love the movie "Dumb and Dumber." However, I don't want to spend my free time – the little that I have – with someone who could play a role in that movie. Thankfully, Aiden was not feeling well that evening. My sister called me and requested that I come get him before dinner was even delivered to our table. For the first time and only time, I am thankful one of my children was not feeling well. I jetted out and never spoke with him again.

There was another interesting date, and not in a good sense of "interesting." A woman with whom I had previously worked had a single male friend to whom she introduced to me through the use of technology. This guy and I initially met over the phone and spoke multiple times for a couple of weeks before meeting in person. He was a nice guy who seemed very gentle and respectful. He had children and really seemed to love them. Of course, this doesn't necessarily mean anything. From my past experiences, I've learned to be cautious of a man's child status and experience.

We planned a day and time to meet. Again, the place we chose is Chili's in Owasso. When I arrived, he was waiting in his car. We both got out of our cars and walked in together. He was shorter than I am which is hard to do, as I'm only 5' 1"! He had about 20 wrinkles around each eye. Wrinkles aren't bad; I have a few. However, the picture he sent me was obviously from about 10 – 15 years ago. While at dinner, he ordered the same thing as me, a grilled chicken Caesar salad. Interesting choice for a guy. After we received our food, we began eating. That's when the train began to derail. He chewed with his mouth open and I saw his food before and after every chomp. I will never again look at grilled chicken Caesar salad the same.

Dating isn't for me. I know this. I mean, I'm not going to go beyond dating with anyone anyway. I just don't trust anyone. I can't trust anyone. And if I'm not interested in building a relationship with someone, why even date?

And while contemplating the aforementioned points, I am reacquainted with someone from high school. We will call him Jesse. Jesse and I were never really friends in school. I knew of him, but we probably only exchanged a short "hello" during our high school years. We connected on MySpace, a great networking site at the time. And while we barely exchanged words in our younger years, just knowing he is from my pre-adult days reminds me of my previous innocence. This feeling is very similar to my feelings about my relationship with Jessica, my friend of many years. When we get together, it's almost as if all my baggage from failed relationships and all the ugly things that have taken place in my life are non-existent. And although it's temporary, lasting but a few hours, it's refreshing.

After reintroducing ourselves to each other via MySpace and talking for a few weeks via phone, Jesse and I decide to meet for dinner. On the way there, I was a little excited… excited to be in the company of someone with no pressure. The weather was perfect, sunny and 85, which seemed to heighten my excitement. Upon arriving, I was greeted by Jesse with a pleasant, warming smile. Over the course of dinner, the conversation was great. He was relaxed. I was relaxed. There was no pressure. We talked a lot. We laughed a lot. It went about as well as it could have gone.

Jesse and I decided to continue our friendship with casual dates each weekend. These dates were simply friendship, nothing more. He began to come to family events as my friend. Every now and then, he would also come over for dinner. My entire family was accepting of Jesse and our spending time together; over several months this resulted in us developing a fondness for one another. At this time in my life, I wasn't sure I was ready to consider anything beyond friendship, especially a more consistent dating relationship. I didn't trust myself to make good choices regarding the men in my life, since my children's father was a drug addict and the next man I married was a sexual predator. Of course I didn't trust myself to make good choices about men with my recent history!

And then God shows up. He's always there, but He shows us the path that He wants us to take or the one He wants us to completely avoid. And, He does it in such a clear, eye opening way. All we have to do is be willing to listen.

As if a switch had been flipped, something changed in Jesse. He suddenly became aggressive and controlling with his words and actions. He demanded to know what I did during the day and with whom I spoke while at work, with whom I had lunch, and with whom I communicated via email, text, and social media. I quickly put on the brakes. I put on the brakes so hard and so quickly, I visualized intense skid marks and smoke in my mind! While I had, prior to these huge, waving red flags, enjoyed Jesse's company, I had to tell him that we couldn't continue to be anything more than friends due to his controlling behavior. I clearly communicated to him that I wasn't going to deal with it, and I didn't have to. He promised not to be controlling and stated he wanted to still be friends. I obliged. We talked every now and then over the next few weeks.

One Saturday, the kids were gone to their dad's house. It was a beautiful day, so I had my windows open. I love the smell of my house when I have fresh air flowing through. I had taken a shower and was in my towel in my bedroom looking through the closet for something to wear. I hear the doorbell ring. I yell out, "Just a minute." The doorbell rang again within a few seconds. I yell out again but louder this time, "Just a minute!" Within seconds, Jesse walked into my room. He had taken the screen off my large window in my living room right next to the front door and climbed into my house. He threw me on my bed. I quickly got up, yelled at him to get out, and threatened to call the police. He grabbed my phone out of my hand and threw it up against the wall, making a gash in the drywall. I started screaming loudly, and he left.

I would like to say that was my last encounter with him, although it's not true. Two weeks later, the kids were at their dad's for weekend visitation again. It was a Friday night, and there was a high school football game up the street. My street served as overflow parking for football games, as the parking area at the field isn't large enough to accommodate all the football fans in my town. It was 10 p.m., and I heard a motorcycle pull up. I thought it sounded like Jesse's, but was confused as to why he would be at my house considering how explosive and ridiculous our last encounter had been. My doorbell rang. Jesse begged me to open the door. Through the door, I told him to leave and never, ever come back, or call me, or text me, or reach out to me via any social media website. I told him I would call the police if he didn't leave. At last, he left. And that was the end of Jesse.

Somehow, I attract the crazies.

For a month or two after that, I kept talking to God about how these crazy, problem-ridden men come into my life, and why I let them. And I communicated with God about how even more so than ever, I just don't trust my ability to choose any man, friend or otherwise, to be a part of my life. And I'll never forget God revealing to me that I could indeed trust myself to choose. I had demonstrated that I could firmly and assertively stand up to anyone who exhibits controlling behavior. I had demonstrated that I could identify controlling behavior the moment it started to rear its ugly head. I had demonstrated that I could swiftly end a relationship that was unhealthy. I suddenly felt empowered... more empowered than in all of the past 8 years. And that empowerment added confidence. And that confidence lightened my heart.

I was finding my new normal. And my new normal suddenly felt really, really good.

13 THE AVERAGE LIFE

It's been 9 months since our trial ended. Ashlyn is now almost 9. Alayna is 7, and Aiden is 5. Ashlyn and Alayna both play softball, though they play on separate teams. It's a juggling act to get them both to practices, but I make it work. And thankfully, their games are at the same softball complex and most often they are at different times so I can watch both games.

Ashlyn does very well in school. She's in 2nd grade and at the top of her class. I always get compliments about how sweet of a girl she is. Ashlyn also has great friendships with others. She's just like all other young girls and enjoys having sleepovers. Because I'm not very trusting of others, I don't allow her to go to her friends' homes often, but I do allow her to have friends over whenever she asks.

Ashlyn's heart has always been huge; she is constantly concerned for others' well being and she always puts others first, so much so that her needs and wants are secondary to everyone else's needs or wants. This is not a result of the incident, as she was like this even before her innocence was stolen from her. I regularly encourage her to do what she wants to do, play with the toys she wants to play with, and quit giving things up for others just because they want them. For example, she often gives her siblings toys with which she is playing simply because they want them. This happens a lot with Aiden as with many other 5 year olds!

Ashlyn rarely speaks of the incident. Every now and then, she'll mention that she's thinking about it. I invite her to share her thoughts, though she doesn't. She just wants me to know she's thinking about it.

I'm learning how to live without thinking about Jack and that nightmare every day. It gets easier and believe it or not, I have days where it doesn't even cross my mind. I've been in the process of understanding who I am, where I fit in, and what my goals are *today*. I've learned how to accept myself and my choices. I've learned how to not take responsibility for others' choices. And I've learned how to enjoy having people in my life.

Growing up, I envisioned being above average in everything – my career, my income, my relationships, my lifestyle, and my overall life. It's not that I wanted to be better than anyone else, but *I* wanted to strive for excellence. I've always wanted to have nice things such as a larger, newer home, a great, newer car, and a lifestyle that allowed me to be in the social scene regularly and have the ability to travel multiple times a year.

Now that I am where I am, I am perfectly fine with living an average lifestyle. I work hard and am definitely an above average producer. The reason, in part, that I want to excel is because I want to be the best in my profession, or at least one of the best. It's also because I am a single mom and know that I have to maintain my position. I have to prove myself and have to be my best every day. However, my home, vehicle, social activities, and ability to travel are average and perhaps even below average. And I'm ok with that. I'm more than ok with that. I'm content. I'm happy. I have peace. And I love my life.

I am an average Joe (or Josetta if you want to be gender specific).

I have incredible friendships, old and new. Jessica and I still communicate every now and again. We always seem to pick up where we left off. I've also developed new friendships with my colleagues. I'm so thankful to know them. And I still have the friendships I've developed over the past 10 years. With my crazy busy schedule of work, kids' activities, and school responsibilities, I'm really only free to see my friends during lunch dates and an occasional dinner. I'll take it!

One of my friendships I've really enjoyed has been with a client of mine, Gregg. He works in an HR department of a national company that is headquartered here in Tulsa. That company has grown tremendously, and as a result, he has need of my professional recruiting expertise. Gregg's company is my largest client. Through working so closely together and talking nearly every day over the past year, we have developed a friendship that is based mostly on sarcasm and numerous accounts of our screwed up experiences. And do we have plenty! Gregg was actually one of the first people I called when I got off the phone with the District Attorney informing me our court case was over. I hadn't spoken much of the situation, though Gregg knew a little about it.

Gregg is divorced without children. He was married for a little over a year when his wife cheated on him. This eventually led them down the all too familiar path for many people of divorce. He seems to be a good guy who doesn't deserve to get pooped on like that. But what do I know? My judge of character has been quite flawed in the past. What's so weird is on a professional level, I can identify red flags with employees, candidates, and even clients early on. But in my personal life, I've been proven wrong in a big way.

Our typical Monday morning consists of a phone call to share our weekend sagas. This time, he shares with me his nightmare of a date with an ex-girlfriend who, after all these years, thinks there is a chance at love again. In fact, when discussing our weekend plans the Friday before, he told me about having arranged this meeting of dinner and a movie. He said they were going as just friends. Though I had warned him. I told him that she was going to spend a lot of time getting ready, hair styled flawlessly and perfectly applied make up. I even told him that she'd dress in her favorite, most flattering outfit and put on a lot of perfume. Gregg denied that she had any romantic thoughts about the two of them. However, our Monday morning conversation proved I was correct! (I love being right probably more than the average person.)

Another Monday morning, Gregg shares with me his story of a girl who, on their first date, comes on so strong that he is quite uncomfortable and decides to never see her again. I think this is a little awkward, and of course, I share these thoughts with him, which are unsolicited by the way. He laughed it off. What can he say!?!

My crazy dating stories consist of the shiny forehead guy, food-smacking guy, and of course Jesse. I also add fun stories of the kids. They are my daily entertainment and they say the craziest things. I love sharing stories about them because I know it brightens not only my day but others' days.

It's been a year since Gregg and I began working together. However, as I have chosen to go to work for another organization in a corporate HR environment, I will no longer be working with him. I'm a little saddened by this, but I know this move is the right move for my career and for my family. I communicate my plans of departure to Gregg, and he is disappointed, just as I am. Without working together, we will no longer have day to day interaction. During my final two weeks, he receives a promotion. So we decided to meet on Friday after work for a celebratory dinner for his promotion and my new job. Since he will no longer be my client, this is not considered a conflict of interest.

Friday arrives and I'm excited about the opportunity to have a non-client/vendor meeting later tonight. Gregg is a friend who appreciates sarcasm as much as I do which is rare. I'm looking forward to the relaxed, fun ambiance of the evening with no pressure and no expectations. We meet up at El Guapo's in downtown Tulsa and request rooftop seating. Fortunately, there is no wait. We talk and talk and talk. I'm sure we are every wait staff's worst nightmare! Our waitress has to circle back around to us multiple times just for our drink order because we are too busy talking to decide what we want! We end up staying there for at least two hours talking and laughing, eating and drinking.

Neither of us is quite ready to part ways, so we decide to go to a trendy bar up the street. We talk and talk for about an hour before Gregg receives a text from a friend of his requesting his presence at a dance club on the other side of town. Gregg asks if I want to join him. It sounds like fun, so what the heck!

I had the best time that night! We sang. We danced. That evening was just what I needed. It's just what my heart needed – light, fun friendship with no pressures. Gregg drove me back to my car, which was still parked, at El Guapo's. We talked for about 45 minutes and at 3 a.m., I finally got into my own car to go home.

Over the next 6 months, Gregg and I decide to start dating. We see each other every weekend after our initial outing. I enjoy his fun, sarcastic personality. I enjoy not having the pressures of expectations. We had a conversation early on in our dating relationship during which we agreed that neither of us had any expectations with the exception that if either of us want to stop seeing the other, we will tell the other. Simple enough.

Three months into the dating relationship, I realize that I really, really like this guy. And because I seem to be a terrible judge of character, I choose to have my family either give me a stamp of approval or tell me to run. So, I arrange a meeting between Gregg and my parents, my sisters, and their husbands. Gregg understands the stakes. He knows that if they pick up on any red flags, our dating relationship will end. He understands he will be under a microscope, yet he agrees to attend.

The get-together goes well. And, I have their approval. Thus begins our relationship.

Over the next two years, I introduce Gregg to my children. They are quite accepting, even Ashlyn. I sense absolutely nothing negative with him. No negative vibes. No red flags. We continue to see each other every weekend and never speak of marriage, as he knows how I feel about this subject. He has even nicknamed me "Ice Princess." It's a title I'll gladly take. I think I've earned it.

I meet Gregg's close friends with whom he's been friends since childhood and early adulthood. They seem normal. I meet his parents and sisters. They all are normal as well. I sense no warning signs, and believe me, I'm looking for them not only with eyes wide open, but with a magnifying glass and with binoculars!

Gregg knows I don't like receiving flowers, although I don't think he knows why. Really, I don't like having flowers delivered to me at work by a complete stranger. For our dating anniversaries and my birthday, he personally delivers flowers to me at work, and I like it. I actually appreciate it. However, I don't want flowers any other time! I don't want flowers "just because." I'd rather have a text message or a voice mail message telling me he's thinking of me.

Gregg respects my time with my kids. He understands that during the week, the evenings are reserved for my kids, their school work, and our family time, and he doesn't try to interfere with that. If we speak on the phone in the evenings, he understands that it's only after the kids go to bed. I appreciate him understanding and respecting those boundaries.

*****

Gregg and I have been dating for two years. Much to my surprise, during the evening after a U2 concert, my absolute all-time favorite band, Gregg proposes. Even until this moment, we haven't discussed the possibility or options of marriage. Much to my ignorance, Gregg has tried in the past to bring up the subject by referencing others getting married and making an example of their experiences. Apparently, I have been completely oblivious. To Gregg's surprise and relief, I said, "Yes!"

And so begins the planning of our lives together. I never thought I'd do this again. But here I am, still with no expectations except to enjoy today… enjoy what I have today.

14 REOPENING THE WOUND

My life is fabulous. I have wonderful children. They are healthy and happy kids. They are each doing well in school and are active in extracurricular activities. I have an incredible man in my life that accepts me for who I am. He allows me to be me. He is trusting *and* trustworthy. He isn't controlling. He isn't jealous. And, he's great to my kids. As a male role model, he fits well into their lives, and he doesn't try to replace their dad. In fact, he doesn't want to replace their dad. Life is as it should be.

And then it happens… I receive a message via social media, from someone with whom I am not familiar. The message reads, "Lisa, you don't know me. But, I would like to talk with you when you have a chance. Thanks." My heart sinks. My intuition tells me that this is about Jack.

I call my dad (because he's the first person I call about anything) to share the details of this message. I share with him my instinct that this has something to do with Jack. I tell him that I think I should call her and be completely honest. He gives me great advice, as always, and explains, "You know what you need to do. You need to call her. You need to tell her the truth." He tells me I need to share Ashlyn's story. He tells me I need to share *our* story.

While cooking dinner, I reluctantly share with Gregg the details of the message I received from Darla, a woman about whom I know nothing. And I hesitantly share with Gregg the reason I believe she is contacting me. Considering we just got engaged and are moving forward with our lives, this timing couldn't be any worse. Gregg understands my desire to call her back and the responsibility I feel. I have to take the time to share my experiences with her.

I'm anxious about the call, yet I can't wait to talk to this stranger. So after dinner, I excuse myself to the back yard where I'm alone. And I call her.

I hear, "Hello, this is Darla." And thus begins the conversation. Darla briefly explains that she met Jack through work and that they dated for close to a year. Throughout their relationship, he often mentioned my name to Darla. During their conversations, Jack told Darla I was a crazy ex-wife who was upset with him for no reason and made up a crazy story about him molesting my daughter. He also told her that I needed to be rescued and that he was the knight in shining armor who rescued me. He told her that I wanted to find someone to pay my expenses and that I actually used him for his financial support. I'm thinking, "What nerve he has!"

Although Jack said I was a crazy ex-wife, Darla said when he talked about me, he wasn't upset or bitter. He talked about me like someone would talk about a friend or sister.

Then, Darla asks me to share with her my experience with Jack. So, I do. I share everything. I briefly share details of my life before I met Jack. I share our beginning and how he truly was a knight in shining armor who swept me off my feet. It's so hard to talk about it now because I was truly in love with Jack at one time. And remembering being in love with him almost makes me feel as though I'm betraying my own daughter, merely by remembering there was a time in which I loved him. Recollecting those feelings also makes me feel unclean; it is a feeling that cannot be washed away. While it really was not that long ago, actually 5 1/2 years, it seems so very long ago and as if it happened to a completely different person. It's as though it wasn't truly me who lived through that, who survived that.

I share with Darla my love for family and how when I was with Jack, I was able to solely focus on my family. I loved taking care of my family. And I loved that taking care of my family was my primary, full-time job. I loved that I had the privilege of staying home to focus on my family. I loved taking care of our home, breakfast and lunch and dinner and the grocery shopping and organizing and volunteering for events at school. I loved scheduling date nights, planning romantic dinners, planning and hosting family gatherings and having relaxing getaways and... And then I realize I'm not in that life anymore. A part of me aches. And the ache is deep, so very deep. It aches deep in my chest. I ache because I miss that life or at least the fantasy in which I was living. And I ache because I feel guilty that I miss that life. It's hard to breathe. It's hard to catch my breath. It's hard to talk. Focusing on my breathing, I take a minute to collect myself just so I can continue.

As tears stream down my face, I begin to explain to Darla how the fall of our life as I knew it began. I describe Jack's controlling and erratic behaviors towards the end. I explain how I had to get out and how quick I actually got us out. I share Ashlyn's anger that led us to counseling, which then led a professional to share with me the details of Ashlyn's story. I explain that as a parent, I did not do the one thing I am supposed to do – I did not protect my child. I have to regularly forgive myself for this. It's tough. It's hard. Satan wants me to feel these feelings of guilt. I have to focus on forgiving... forgiving myself.

I detail the entire, ridiculously long court process. I share the details of his light, unfair conviction. And I explain the process of rebuilding our life since then.

It's definitely been a process. It's definitely taken some time to heal and a focus on moving forward.

Darla tells me she has a daughter with the same name and the same initials as my Ashlyn. And these two Ashlyns are only 6 weeks apart in age. As she begins to share her story, I become infuriated! I go from grieving the loss of my fantasy life to grieving my daughter's experience to being livid at what a sick bastard this guy really is! As sexual predators do, he had groomed my entire family, and he was now grooming Darla's!

And now, I want justice. All over again, I want justice! I don't even know it yet, but I'm about to hear how justice has been served!

Darla explains that several months ago, Jack had to go back to court to basically "check in" for probation purposes. Up until this court hearing, he didn't have to check in inside a courtroom. He requested Darla's presence as well as his oldest daughter's presence there that day. He actually insisted they stay in the lobby right outside the courtroom. At the conclusion of his court hearing, Jack's attorney took Jack's watch and wallet to Darla and Jack's daughter and explained he would not be returning home with them. He was going to prison. Darla explains how shocked she was and how she just didn't understand.

As of today, they are still together. Darla is reaching out to me for answers, for the truth. And I have given her not only what she wants, but what she deserves.

I plan to get the rest of the truth at the courthouse on Monday!

*****

It's Monday. On my lunch break from work, I go to the courthouse to inquire about the reasons Jack's suspended sentence was accelerated. I purchase copies of the documents of his latest court appearance. And here in the documents, all is stated in black and white. 1) Knowingly having phone sex with a minor female. This was the determining factor for his sentence being accelerated. Of course, I could have told them that he was a sick man who would continue his sick ways. There were also other instances where already he violated his suspended sentence such as 2) breaking curfew, 3) viewing pornography online, 4) entering a bar, 5) taking a controlled substance not prescribed to him, and 6) leaving Tulsa county. Apparently, all of these things had been exposed previously during his required monthly polygraph test.

I had no idea the terms of his probation included a curfew and inability to leave Tulsa county! And knowing those terms gives me comfort that although he didn't immediately go to prison, he did suffer. What grown man wants to deal with such rules as a daily curfew of 10 p.m., the inability to leave the county in which he lives and works, the restriction of surfing the internet, or even being prevented from entering any school to watch his kids play sports? Not only did Jack have these rules, but he also had to register as a sex offender. This registered sex offender label is detailed on his driver's license. It shows up on any background check that any potential employer runs on him. It's public record for his neighbors to see. I'm sure he hasn't had it easy since his conviction. And I'm glad for that.

Of course, after reviewing the reasons, in black and white, that ultimately lead to Jack's imprisonment, I immediately contact Darla for her fax number. I send these reports directly to her. She is in shock, understandably so. And her life, like my life five and a half years earlier, immediately begins to crumble. All she knows about Jack up to this point has been a lie. She questions everything about him and all that they were together. Then, she realizes that she invited this monster into her life and allowed him to be around her children. She begins questioning herself and all that she thought she knew about herself. She questions her ability to identify good people from bad people. Suddenly, she doesn't trust anyone or anything. And then the grieving process begins.

Darla wonders how she is going to tell her children. She wonders *if* she should tell her children. She wonders if he ever did anything inappropriate to her daughter. She wonders how she is going to tell her dad and her sisters. She wonders how she is going to get through the afternoon at work. She's angry, angry with herself. She's also very angry with Jack. She's sad. She's relieved that she finally has the truth and that it's over. She's confused. She feels nauseous. Her life seems to be spinning out of control. She knows she has to get it together and keep it together. She wonders how she is going to interact with Jack now. She knows she has to end her relationship with him. She wonders how to end it. She starts on the rollercoaster of emotions with which I am all too familiar. My heart hurts for her. And my heart hurts again for me. And my heart hurts again for Ashlyn.

My wound has reopened. When the wound healed previously, it healed without being properly cleansed. It healed with infection still living in it. It healed with unforgiveness for myself, though I just didn't know it until now. Now that it's reopened, I feel the infection. I feel the unforgiveness, and I feel the anger. I feel the emotions of being desperate and alone, trying to survive this moment just so that I can get to the next moment to try to survive that one. I feel the rawness of it all as if it happened yesterday.

Now that the wound is reopened, I will choose to make a change. I will choose to clean it out. Now, I can allow it to heal as it should. It can heal as I deserve for it to heal. It can heal as my Ashlyn, Alayna, and Aiden deserve for it to heal. I can be the mom that God intends for me to be to my precious children. Gregg also deserves for my heart to heal so that I can be the wife to him that God intends me to be. It can heal as it should so that I can be the witness for God as He intends for me to be, for His kingdom.

15 UNWELCOME VISITS

Darla and I have been meeting regularly over lunch during the week and sometimes for brunch on Saturdays just to talk through the nightmare of this madness. We laugh. We cry. We know how the other one feels, losing ourselves to love, for someone who turned out to be a pedophile. We believed it was love at the time. Now, we feel relieved to know the truth. However, we feel disgusted that we could have ever shared ourselves intimately on any and all levels with a pedophile and that we actually invited this pedophile into our families and worst of all, among our precious, innocent children. We often talk about our difficulty trusting others. We talk about the difficulty we have in making choices – all choices – even as small as what to order at a restaurant.

Darla is in survival mode at this moment, and for once, through this entire horrendous reality through which I've lived, I do not feel alone. I don't have to be strong in front of anyone. I can let it all out with Darla. She gets it. She understands. She knows the shame I feel sharing any part of my life with this monster because she feels the same shame. She knows the distrust I have of myself and others. She has the same distrust of herself and others. Darla is trying to put back together a life that is shattered into a million little pieces. I had to do that, and now since I received that first message from Darla, I find myself doing it again. All the pain has resurfaced, and

I'm reliving the nightmare through these all-consuming memories.

Through our conversations, I learn about the Jack she knew. While Jack and I were very active and planted in church, he and Darla didn't attend church often. They visited my campus of Life.Church once, but Jack stated he didn't like seeing a pastor on a screen; he explained to Darla he preferred the pastor being present at the church in person, and said he didn't want to go there again. They didn't return. They visited a few other churches, but did not attend regularly.

With Darla, Jack was quiet and more of a homebody. He didn't enjoy going places. My experience with Jack was quite different. He enjoyed being out. He enjoyed listening to live music while partaking in a few drinks (and sometimes more than a few drinks). He enjoyed going out to dinner. While married, we went on dates regularly. We took the family out often. We were at church and Sunday school every weekend and attended many church events. Whether at work, church, or out with me, Jack was the suave, charming guy wherever he went. He was debonair with a boyish innocence about him. Middle-aged women loved him. Older women adored him.

None of those women could have imaged he was capable of such a heinous crime.

Since meeting Darla, I check oscn.net regularly to confirm that Jack is still in prison. Unfortunately, however, I discover that his release date has been moved up by a year. A YEAR! I don't understand how they could move up his release date by a year, especially since neither the court nor the prison have notified me or my family. I thought they notified the victim and the victim's family to give them an opportunity to make a statement when a prisoner was up for the option of being released. But they didn't.

*****

It's Sunday, and I know that Jack was released from prison a week and a half ago. Since his release, I have literally been on edge, looking behind me and around me everywhere I go. I am scared I am going to see him somewhere; maybe the grocery store, maybe the coffee shop, maybe in the car next to me at the stoplight. I wonder how I would react to him if I saw him. Would I yell at him? Would I be paralyzed with fear? Would I run away? I wish he was still in prison so that I didn't have to contemplate such things.

However, with it being Sunday, I am going to focus on the message at church, serving the three year olds in the class Gregg and I teach, and being with my family the rest of the day. God did not give us a spirit of fear. I refuse to let Jack consume my thoughts or steal my peace.

I'm so thankful for a safe place to worship. The message was phenomenal, as always! Gregg and I are taking a break between the message and our class of three year olds. During this time, the kids like to take a break from church as well. They get out of their classes and grab drinks and snacks for 20 minutes before the next experience begins.

I run to the restroom quickly before I have to report to teach the precious 3 year olds. As I am exiting the restroom, there he is. There is Jack! Jack is at my church! He is at the church that he rejected a few years ago when he attended with Darla. I gasp. I can't breathe. I am shaking. My heart is racing. I don't want him to see the fear I feel. He's not supposed to be here. This is MY church. Where's Ashlyn? And Alayna and Aiden? I have to make sure Ashlyn doesn't see him. What about the other children here at the church? He shouldn't be around any children! No children are safe here. He has violated my space, my place of comfort. I am running to try to find the LifeKIDS pastor, Ashlie.

Where is she? I have to report him! I find her. I am spewing information; I just hope she can keep up! I tell her he's here! Jack is here! I had told her about Jack a few weeks ago. The timing of that conversation was all God's doing. I understand that now.

I find Gregg to let him know about Jack. He finds the kids and ensures they are safe and gets them back to class safely and without seeing Jack. Thank God!

My head is spinning. Why is he here? Why won't he leave me

alone? I no longer feel safe. I feel as though my children are no longer safe. I'm furious that I'm still scared of him. I'm livid that he came to intimidate me. I'm angry that I even have to deal with him again. I'm livid that I don't have a choice in this and that I'm forced to deal with him again.

Over the next week, I am in continuous contact with the Ashlie, the LifeKIDS pastor. I send her photos of him so that she can easily recognize him if he ever returns. She shares the photos with the other pastors at the church so they can each identify him as well.

Ashlie calls a Tulsa Police Officer who works security for a large church in the city to ask him if he's ever experienced something like this. The police officer asks Ashlie for the name of the man who came to our church. She gives him Jack's name, and immediately the police officer explains that Jack is banned from their church. They even have photos of him in their office so that they can quickly recognize him to escort him out of the building. Jack's kids attend a Christian school in Tulsa, and they sometimes play sports in this church's gymnasium. (This church also has a private school of its own.) Although Jack is a registered sex offender and is not allowed in schools, he has tried to sneak in and attend his kids' games. Each time, he's been escorted out and told not to return. Ashlie shares this conversation with me, and it confirms how sick and dangerous he is.

During conversations with Ashlie, I learn that registered sex offenders cannot attend a church without first talking to administration and divulging their sex offender status, requesting permission to attend, and then being granted permission to attend. This is part of the sex offender guidelines. All sex offenders know this (or should know this). However, Jack has lived his life as though rules don't apply to him. I'm not surprised that he once again does not follow rules and guidelines even though, in this case, it's the law.

In addition to providing photos of Jack to people at church, I also have to go to Ashlyn's school and explain the situation to the administration as well as provide them with photos of Jack. I need to ensure everyone is safe if he does show up at their school.

Throughout the week, I'm constantly worried about the kids walking home from the bus stop. Although I've moved to a different house since I originally moved to this town, I'm worried that Jack may know where I live and try to intimidate the kids simply by sitting in his car and watching them as they walk home after they get off the bus. I'm scared Jack might come to my house. I'm worried that Jack might break into my house. What if he breaks in when the kids are at school and is inside, waiting for them when they get home from school? I work 30 minutes away from home. I couldn't possibly get home quick enough to save them. I fear Jack might follow us and make his presence known wherever we go whether it's the grocery store or even the kids' sporting events. But, I know our God doesn't give us a spirit of fear; I must remind myself over and over again.

A week has passed since Jack came to our church. Hesitantly, I take my family to church. I refuse to let Jack keep us from our church home. I've been praying that we don't see Jack. I'm nervous as I walk through the doors. My stomach is in knots. My chest is heavy. My heart is racing. I am even sweating.

As I escort the kids to their class, I look all around for that familiar face. My eyes are scanning over everyone ahead of me, next to me, behind me. I'm quickly glancing at everyone in the crowd, nervous that I might see him.

I safely and without incident get the kids to class. Gregg and I grab a tea (our usual) and walk into the experience room (where the message is given). We are seated. Whew! No catastrophes!

I sing my heart out during praise and worship. (I love, love, love to sing, but am definitely not going to lead anyone to Jesus with my singing abilities, or lack thereof!) I'm so thankful that He protected us.

The lights are super dim, and the experience room is quite dark. The message begins. Pastor Craig is on the screen. He is an incredible leader, speaker, and teacher. He truly captivates the attention of those who attend his sermons. I love seeing all the work

God is doing through Pastor Craig! As always, Gregg and I are entrenched in the message. We're taking notes. We're learning more about the Word of God. And then…

Fifteen minutes into the message, the Worship Pastor approaches us at our seats. He explains that Jack came to the church again and that we need to step out to talk with a police officer. Once again, I'm in a state of shock. As we exit the experience room and enter the lobby, I ask for the information to be repeated. I was once again told that Jack came to the church again today and that we need to speak with a police officer. This is all almost too much to process. It's too much to comprehend.

We are escorted to a back office. I'm shaking. I'm crying. (As you know, I usually never cry in public.) The police officer tells Gregg and me that Jack came in the lobby and was immediately recognized by staff members and the police officer who is always present at our church. Jack walked right into the men's restroom. Two police officers quickly followed behind and arrested him for 1) attending church without first being granted permission to do so from church administration and 2) entering a school. (Our church is a portable church that has its service in a school, though we'll be transitioned to our own building once construction is complete.)

The police officer explains that I need to provide a written statement about last week's experience and then document Jack's return to the church this week. The police officer also requests that I provide facts about Jack's conviction of sexually assaulting my daughter. I also include in my statement that Jack hates Life.Church (based on his opinion when he and Darla attended several years ago) and that he is only there to intimidate me and my family.

After completing my written statement, I'm still in disbelief; this can't be happening. I'm so thankful that everyone on staff and the police officers responded so quickly and without incident. I thank God that I didn't see him. I thank God that my children didn't see him. Most importantly, I'm so thankful that Ashlyn didn't have to face him.

Knowing that Jack has been arrested and is in jail makes me feel safe. I will sleep better tonight than I have during the past week.

Although Jack is in jail and for the moment I'm protected, I have to request a protective order. This process takes half a day. As if I don't have anything better to do! Half a day of vacation, wasted on this. I go to DVIS and fill out the paperwork; I need to attempt to get some sort of piece of paper that documents that my family and I are protected from this man. I appreciate the advocate at DVIS and the judge that listens to my case. I'm even more grateful that I'm granted an emergency protective order. I go back in two weeks for the permanent protective order. Let's hope he doesn't show up to fight it. Surely he won't.

Several days after the incident at church, the arresting police officer calls me. He advises me to file a stalking report. He explains that he has no doubt that Jack was stalking me based on conversations that transpired after Jack was arrested. After being arrested, Jack told the officer that Life.Church was his church. However, when Jack's adult children arrived at the police station, the police officer asked Jack's children if Life.Church was their dad's church. Jack's children said no. They confirmed that Life.Church is indeed *not* Jack's church.

I arrive at the Owasso Police Department to file the stalking report as advised by police officer. Everyone at the Owasso Police Department is so helpful and supportive and makes this process as easy as it possibly can be. I provide every detail that I am able, including Jack's criminal case number from when he sexually assaulted my daughter. I do this so that they can easily reference the details of his conviction. I also explain in my written statement that during his sentencing, Jack was ordered to never contact me or my family again and to stay away from us. In addition to my statements, the police officers contacted Darla to obtain a statement from her in order to complete the stalking report. In her statement, she confirms that Jack stated he didn't like Life.Church and that he never wanted to return.

The stalking report has now been filed. There should be sufficient documentation and proof in this stalking report for the district attorney to do something.

Now we wait.

16 REBUILDING WITHOUT FEAR

I haven't heard anything since I filed the stalking report. I contact the Owasso Police Department for an update. They haven't heard anything from the Tulsa County District Attorney's office. The police officer advises us that he will contact the DA's office and then contact me with any news he obtains.

A few days later, I receive a call from the police officer explaining that the DA's office chose not to file any charges against Jack. So, let me get this straight. Jack is a registered sex offender and breaks several rules all sex offenders must follow: 1) He went into a school and 2) he attended church without first obtaining clearance from the church administration. 3) Not only did he break several rules that sex offenders must follow, he also blatantly disregarded the orders the judge gave him during his sentencing to stay away from me and my family. Jack once again thinks rules don't apply to him. And our system is so messed up that it lets him get away with it.

Who's protected here? Not my precious daughter. Not me. Not my family. There are absolutely no consequences for Jack.

I communicate my disgust to the police officer. I also communicate my repulsion to another police officer who is a personal friend. This friend shares a story with me of another time where he saw the system respond unjustly. A fellow police officer had been assaulted by a man. Another police officer witnessed the assault. They arrested the man. They wrote a lengthy police report with complete details of the incident. They provided the report to the District Attorney. However, the DA failed to file charges. Actually, the DA chose not to file charges. Why? How could the DA *not* file charges? This is asinine! (I use that word in honor of my dad. He has used that word for as long as I remember.)

The police officer explains it's all about politics. He says that the DA chooses to file charges on cases that are easy to win, ones that are basically slam dunk cases. See, when the DA is up for re-election, he wants to be able to say, "I have won 98% of all cases filed." So, when the DA chooses whether or not to file criminal charges, the decision is made with political intentions. The victim is not considered in the decision. The victim's safety is definitely not taken into account. If it was, don't you think someone in a position of authority in the court system would have done everything they could to protect my daughter?

Being re-elected; that was the motivation in consideration of whether or not to take action on the police report and my stalking report. Being re-elected was the goal of the Tulsa County DA (in 2010) who chose not to file charges against Jack. This DA chose, for the sake of his own political career, to not protect my daughter against the one man who sexually assaulted her, a convicted registered sex offender. The DA's message to my daughter is, "Getting re-elected is my priority, not you. My being DA is more important to me than your protection." And I'm disgusted at that!

The DA sends the message to other registered sex offenders, "Violate your rules as a registered sex offender without consequences." I'm disgusted at that as well!

Something else I'm disgusted with is the realization that Jack's registered sex offender status expires in April 2017. He has sexually violated two girls (that we know about), yet after April 2017, he will no longer have to register as a sex offender.

So now what? What's our plan to move forward from here? I will tell you. I refuse to live with anger. I refuse to live in fear. God did not give us a spirit of fear but of power, love, and a sound mind. I pray for God to help me with this daily… and sometimes hourly, or even minute by minute. I will not fear. I will have peace.

*****

I have peace. I have joy. My peace and joy do not come from anyone other than my wonderful, ever-present God. My trust is in Him.

And after dating for 2 ½ years, Gregg and I are married. He's been wonderfully supportive through the chaos that is my life. When others would have run, or rather sprinted, from this chaos, he chose to stay. He must be as crazy as I am, to choose to undertake life with me. He has a choice, you know. I am grateful. Not only does he stay, but he provides the ultimate loving, gentle support for me and for my kids.

We try to do all we can to foster growth in my children in all areas – academically, athletically, socially, and spiritually. It takes a village, and man, do we have a village! Remember when I first moved to this town, I utterly hated and despised it? Well, now I absolutely love it! We have remarkable teachers who pour their energy and resources into my children to help them learn and succeed. My children have amazing coaches who do so much more than coach a sport; they are actually molding my children's character and work ethic and teaching them about discipline and integrity. My children have incredible pastors and youth leaders at our church, Life.Church, who impact them in a big way. They speak life into my kids and their consistent, encouraging presence is immeasurable. My parents, Lon's parents, and Gregg's parents have loved my children unconditionally and have laid a great foundation for our family.

My children also have their dad. After legal struggles of his own, he is now sober. He's learning his way through this parenting thing. Aren't we all?!? I'm thankful for his legal struggles, as I don't believe he would be sober without going through them. He would also agree. Lon, Gregg, and I all co-parent beautifully together. In fact, when Lon attends the kids' sports or school functions, he sits next to

Gregg. They talk more to each other than to me. And I'm ok with that.

We all have high expectations of the children. And while I expect their best, I also allow them to fail. After all, aren't failures where we seem to learn the most? My desire is to help guide my children through their failures now so that they can deal with failures as an adult. My hope is that by learning to be more open and honest about their failures, they will be able to share them with me and with others; they don't have to experience them alone. I know I am their biggest cheerleader, and I will always be. I must say they are each incredible human beings with incredible hearts, intellect, and determination. I am so proud of each one of them.

*****

Because Ashlyn has been struggling academically for the last few years, I choose to have her undergo testing to determine if she has any type of learning disability. The test results prove she has Mixed Expressive Receptive Language Disorder. It's essentially a processing disorder. The doctor diagnosing this disorder informs me that it was caused by trauma to Ashlyn's brain as a result of the sexual assault she endured. I'm devastated for her. She has gone through years of school with this disorder. I had no idea.

Prior to the diagnosis, some teachers had suggested Ashlyn hadn't been paying attention in class. Other teachers assumed Ashlyn wasn't trying as hard as she could. Some teachers said she was too chatty and social in class. That's not the case at all. She's had difficulty processing the information while listening during teacher's lectures and through reading her lessons. And she's had difficulty organizing her thoughts for output in assignments, projects, and even being called on in class. Once again, I think about Jack and how every now and then, he seems to creep back into my life. His ugly head rears itself again. Sometimes, I hate him for this. Hasn't Ashlyn had enough hardships in her life already!?! Why does she have to deal with yet another challenge? And then I remember, God won't waste our hurts. God will use our hurts and our challenges if we allow Him to. From these experiences, Ashlyn and I believe we were called to help others.

Ashlyn has been put on an individualized educational plan (IEP). This allows modifications on her assignments, tests, and even interactions with the teachers during class. The IEP is designed to allow Ashlyn the same opportunities, as a result of the modifications, as her fellow students with academic success. Although Ashlyn has some great teachers, other teachers do not want to follow the IEP. Ultimately, Ashlyn doesn't experience success during the first semester on her IEP, which happens to be the first semester of her freshman year in high school. So, I withdraw her and we start homeschooling at her request.

Through two years of homeschooling, Ashlyn has experienced tremendous achievements! Her test scores have improved dramatically. She has also explored drama, which she has always wanted to do. She has been in two plays in Tulsa's drama group for homeschooled students. I loved seeing her on stage! Ashlyn has also joined a co-op and has taken art and journalism classes. God has gifted Ashlyn with astonishing artistic talents. She has drawn a self-portrait that is absolutely mind-blowing! Her favorite, though, is drawing dream catchers. Though she is not one ounce Native American, she has a love for and fascination of dream catchers. Her drawings of them are remarkable!

Ashlyn's confidence is as high as it's been since the sexual assault 10 years ago. I believe this is the perfect timing to re-enroll her in school. I am not the most fabulous teacher (believe it or not), and I don't feel as though I'm the best person to teach Ashlyn for her last two years of high school. Remember, I hate math. It's definitely a weakness. I have avoided teaching Ashlyn geometry, and that's not fair to her. After talking with Ashlyn and after doing much research on the best option for her education, I enroll her in online school through Oklahoma Connections Academy to complete her junior and senior years of high school. So far, all is going well. She is learning the discipline it takes to complete the work on her own. She is experiencing the feeling of accomplishment as she works hard for herself and her future. I am so proud of how she has overcome such adversity. She's only 17 and has lived through much more than many people do in an entire lifetime.

I believe Ashlyn's overall improvement is in part due to her fabulous counselor, Liz. Over the years, we have have sought counseling at different times, but never found a counselor with which Ashlyn connected. That was until Liz. Liz challenges Ashlyn to be the best she can be while giving her support and encouragement. She helps Ashlyn develop and strengthen her critical thinking skills. Liz also empowers Ashlyn to make decisions that are best for her and her future. She believes in and genuinely cares about Ashlyn. And Liz relates to Ashlyn on a level that I have never seen with any other counselor. She has truly been a Godsend.

In addition to school, Ashlyn is involved in the Tulsa Youth Rowing Association (TYRA). The coaches are encouraging and speak life into her. They believe in her. She needs that. She needs others to believe in her. In TYRA, she is challenged, and she works hard. She has great teammates who work hard alongside her. They also challenge her to improve. They are all such selfless teammates. TYRA exemplifies all that it means to be a team. It's been perfect for Ashlyn. I'm so thankful for TYRA.

Our family has added a precious little boy, Zane, who has brought an interesting dynamic to our family. His presence has definitely enriched our lives. Aiden has been asking for a baby brother for several years. And now he has one! Alayna is excited about him as well, but prefers to be more hands-off. Since Zane's birth, Ashlyn has been quite motherly. She loves him and even refers to him as "my kid." She is so caring and loving with him. And he adores her. At the age of 3, Zane prefers Ashlyn over me. Actually, he's preferred her over me since birth. And I'm ok with that.

We have rebuilt our lives. We no longer live in fear. We are living in peace, faith, and love. Are we doing everything right? No. Do we make mistakes? Yes. But we have incredible peace that only comes from God. And we have faith that He will continue to lead our family. We have immeasurable love for each other that endures all things. My cup runneth over.

17 FORGIVENESS

If anyone would have told me 12 years ago that I would go through hell, watch my daughter go through hell, and survive it all to help others as they experience the same nightmare, I would have thought that person was cray-cray! It's a good thing I didn't know!

I have watched God use Ashlyn's story to help others. While writing each chapter in this book, I made various posts on social media such as, "Writing another chapter." I would then receive texts, private messages, or emails me asking what my book was about. People would even ask me about my book when they saw me out and about in the community, at sporting events, and even at business meetings. When I briefly shared Ashlyn's story with those who asked, more often than not they shared their story with me, which was all too familiar. Either they or someone close to them had experienced sexual abuse and most often by someone they knew. Some people explained to me that they had never told anyone and had been holding that pain in for years. Some told me they shared their story with someone as a child, and no one believed them, so they kept it a secret until disclosing it to me. I'm so thankful that each of those people felt comfortable to share it with me because it means the healing process can finally begin for them. Ultimately, what I found is that talking about it seemed to be quite cleansing for them. And from experience, I know talking about it is therapeutic.

Too many people don't talk about it. But I do. And Ashlyn does. We did nothing wrong. We refuse to feel shame.

I have sought out people who have just found themselves in this terrible tragedy trying to make sense of it, trying to survive the day, and sometimes just trying to survive the hour or even the minute. I help give hope to the moms of children who have become victims of child predators. I have made phenomenal friendships through the process. People don't ask for this to happen to them or to their loved ones. However, there can be happiness on the other side of it when we allow God to work through our lives, using the bad experiences for good and for His glory. We just have to be willing to allow God to do it. We have to be open to it. We have to be obedient.

Here's the thing. God has big plans for Ashlyn. I don't know if I believe that God allowed all of this to happen with Jack. What I do know is that He doesn't waste a hurt. I also believe that God knew that if anyone was going to try to stop Jack from hurting others, it was us.

I have learned we also have to be obedient with forgiving. God calls us to forgive others just as He has forgiven us. Matthew 6:14-15 says, "14 For if you forgive other people when they sin against you, your heavenly Father will also forgive you. 15 But if you do not forgive others their sins, your Father will not forgive your sins." Let that sink in for a moment. If we forgive others who sin against us, our Father will also forgive us when we sin. However, if we do not forgive others when they sin against us, our Father will not forgive us of our sins. Incredibly powerful, isn't it?

Let me tell you something else that is quite powerful. Before I was even familiar with this verse (I'm not a Bible scholar!), Ashlyn started the forgiveness process on her own. She felt called to start forgiving Jack. In fact, a few years ago after she started to forgive Jack, Pastor Craig at Life.Church had a message about forgiveness. He referenced Matthew 6:14-15. Here's what is incredibly amazing! Ashlyn's molester's name is actually *Matthew*. (Jack is a nickname I used to help me cope. It might be an abbreviation of a not-so-nice word.) Matthew molested Ashlyn at *the age of 6*. Between the ages of *14 and 15*, she felt it on her heart to forgive him, and she chose to start the process of actually forgiving him. Do you see the significance for Ashlyn of *Matthew 6:14-15*? Since that very day, this has been Ashlyn's scripture. She identifies with it. She has adopted it as her very own, personal scripture. I admire Ashlyn for her strength to forgive. I admire her for her wisdom and obedience to follow God's direction to forgive.

I mess up every single day. Yet, I want to be forgiven. I ask for forgiveness. And although Jack hasn't asked Ashlyn or me for forgiveness, we are still called to forgive him. Ten years ago, forgiveness seemed impossible. Yet, as I began the forgiveness process, I simply forgave Jack because I knew that God couldn't work on him as long as I held onto the bitterness and anger. And when I say "work on him," I mean that God couldn't punish him for what he had done. That's how I felt then.

While that's a start, there's so much more to forgiveness. As I work through the process of forgiving, I experience more peace. With deeper stages of forgiveness, I no longer want God to punish Jack for his wrongdoing. I pray God helps me forgive Jack. I pray that God helps me not have feelings of anger toward Jack. I pray that Jack no longer has feelings, desires, or urges to harm children. I pray for Jack's kids and pray that they and their families are healthy and happy and good citizens in their communities. I pray they have a personal relationship with God. I pray all is well for them. I don't pray these things for Jack yet. I may get there someday.

And then it happens. Something takes me back to the nightmare. It could be a song or a smell or the mention of a restaurant we frequented. It could be a conversation with Darla. It could be seeing Ashlyn struggle as a result of her Mixed Expressive Receptive Language Disorder, at school, or even just understanding someone in a conversation. Then, I feel anger. I feel infuriated. Yet I have to forgive him again. And I go through the process of forgiving again, sometimes daily, though now it doesn't take quite as long. Forgiveness is a process, and with God's grace and guidance, it can be done.

Ashlyn allows God to work through her. She listens to His prompting and shares her story with others when she feels called to do so. She provides a listening ear and empathizes with others who have suffered such tragedy. She embraces them. She gives them hope. She is a light to them. And her light shines ever so bright. Ashlyn is absolutely incredible. She is beautiful. Her soul is beautiful. Her gentle spirit is beautiful. Her love for others is beautiful. Her concern for others is admirable. Ashlyn is going to do great things. God makes all things work together for our good as stated in Romans 8:28. And He's going to do great things through Ashlyn. He already is. He's not going to waste this hurt. He's created a phenomenal, loving, sweet, precious, beautiful, and wonderful person in Ashlyn. I can't wait to see what He has planned for her life. Her story is no longer about happened to her, but is about all that she is doing and will do making a difference in the lives of others.

I can't wait to see what God has planned for Alayna, Aiden, and Zane! This experience has been a family experience. Every single person in our family has been impacted by this. Alayna and Aiden have been incredibly supportive, although when Ashlyn's story was first told years ago, they were so young and couldn't quite comprehend it all. Yet, now, they understand. Their hearts are so soft for others. Their concern for others extends far beyond many teens their age. God is going to do great things through their lives. I'm so excited to see His plans unfold through their journeys.

I'm living God's plan for my life. I attend Life.Church and participate in a Chazown event regularly. Chazown is essentially God's purpose for our lives. Our Chazown is created through a combination of our personal experiences, our core values, and our spiritual gifts. Every single one of us has a Chazown. Only I can fulfill God's unique purpose for my life. Only you can fulfill God's unique purpose for your life.

This is my Chazown. Helping others through this nightmare is my Chazown. I will help others through Ashlyn's story of faith, hope, perseverance, justice, triumph, and forgiveness. And I will continue to live it until the day God says I'm finished and calls me home.

Made in the USA
Middletown, DE
10 July 2016